DRY ROT

DRY ROT

by John Chapman

WARNER CHAPPELL PLAYS

LONDON

A Warner Music Group Company

DRY ROT
First published in 1956
by Warner Chappell Plays Ltd
(pka English Theatre Guild Ltd)
129 Park Street, London W1Y 3FA

Second edition 1985
Third edition 1995

Copyright © John Chapman 1954

ISBN 0 85676 053 6

Dry Rot was first presented by Rix Theatrical Productions on 31st August, 1954 at the Whitehall Theatre, London, with the following cast:

Colonel Wagstaff	Charles Cameron
Mrs Wagstaff	Cicely Paget-Bowman
Beth	Hazel Douglas
Susan Wagstaff	Diana Calderwood
John Danby	John Chapman
Fred Phipps	Brian Rix
Alfred Tubbe	John Slater
Flash Harry	Basil Lord
Albert Polignac	Larry Noble
Sergeant Fire	Wynne Clark

Directed by Wallace Douglas
Designed by Rhoda Gray

The play takes place in the lounge hall of the *Bull and Cow*, a country hotel.

ACT ONE

Scene One	The lounge hall, morning.
Scene Two	The same. Three days later.

ACT TWO

Scene One	The same. The early hours of the following morning.
Scene Two	The same. Eight hours later.
Scene Three	The same. That afternoon.

Photo from the original production at the Whitehall Theatre, London.

ACT ONE

The play takes place in the lounge hall of the BULL AND COW, *a country hotel run by a retired Indian Army Colonel and his wife* (COLONEL AND MRS WAGSTAFF), *and the maid,* BETH BARTON, *a country girl from the West of England.*

Downstage R. *is the fireplace;* U.R. *French windows. In the centre of the back wall a small flight of stairs leads up to a landing and the corridor goes off to the left. Immediately under the landing is the front door. There is a door to the kitchen* D.L. *and one to the dining room* U.L. *On the back wall both* L. *and* R. *of front door are windows. Between the kitchen door* D.L. *and the dining- room door* U.L. *there is a small bar. Between the dining-room and the front door there is a panel which opens in the wall.*

It is morning.

As the CURTAIN RISES, COLONEL WAGSTAFF *appears on the balcony landing in his shirt, trousers, and dressing gown. He calls.*

WAGSTAFF	Doris! (*He gets no reply so exits*).
	(MRS WAGSTAFF *enters from the kitchen with tray laid for breakfast and a paper. She puts it on the table and calls.*)
MRS W	Henry! (*She gets no reply so exits.*)
	(COLONEL WAGSTAFF *enters without dressing gown, putting on his scarf.*)
WAGSTAFF	Doris! (*He exits*).
	(MRS WAGSTAFF *enters with another tray.*)
MRS W	Henry! (*Goes* U.S. *under balcony to get a chair.*)
	COLONEL WAGSTAFF *enters putting on his jacket.*
WAGSTAFF	Doris!!
MRS W	Yes, dear?
WAGSTAFF	Oh, there you are. (*Comes downstairs.*)
MRS W	Yes, Henry. Are you awake yet?
WAGSTAFF	(*mildly sarcastic*). No, dear, sleep walking.
MRS W	Come and have your breakfast.
WAGSTAFF	How long have you been up?

MRS W	Ages. I did all the chores while you were still snoring.
WAGSTAFF	I never snore.
MRS W	No, dear. Here's your newspaper.
WAGSTAFF	Thanks. Anyway, I don't see why you should have to cope. What on earth do we pay Beth for?
MRS W	She's not very well to-day. She had another 'turn' in the night.
WAGSTAFF	What, again. She seems to spend her whole life revolving.
MRS W	Now stop grumbling, Henry, and get on with your breakfast.
WAGSTAFF	I used to think the servants we had in India were pretty bad, but Beth takes the biscuit. I don't know how the previous owners put up with her.
MRS W	Perhaps they couldn't, and that's why they left.
WAGSTAFF	Been easier to get rid of her, wouldn't it?
MRS W	It's very difficult to get through to her. They may have thought it simpler in the long run to move themselves.
WAGSTAFF	I'll get through if I have to blast.
MRS W	Yes, dear. What's in the paper, anything startling?
WAGSTAFF	No, not a thing, might just as well be yesterday's.
MRS W	Well, that's something to be thankful for. (*Looks over his shoulder.*) Oh, it is yesterday's. Beth must have put the wrong one out.
WAGSTAFF	It is just possible. (*Calls.*) Beth!
MRS W	Oh, don't call her now, Henry, she's in the middle of washing up. (*Gets another paper from table by front door.*)

WAGSTAFF	Beth! (*Crash of crockery off stage.*)
MRS W	I told you she was washing up.
WAGSTAFF	I always seem to catch her in mid-air.
MRS W	Anyway, here it is. (*Gives him the paper.*)
	(*Enter* BETH, *a gawky West Country girl.*)
BETH	'Ave you done?
WAGSTAFF	Done? Done what?
BETH	With the tray.
WAGSTAFF	Not yet.
BETH	Well 'urry. (*Pushes her face into the Colonel's.*) Oi can't hang around here all day.
WAGSTAFF	Good!
MRS W	Henry!
WAGSTAFF	Any letters this morning?
MRS W	I haven't seen any.
BETH	I haven't seen none neither.
WAGSTAFF	Pity, I was hoping we might have some people here for race week.
MRS W	We shall have them soon enough. After all it's quite early in the season, and people weren't likely to come here during the winter.
WAGSTAFF	True. (*Reads his paper again.*)
BETH	Arr, and its gets proper cold in the winter, don't it?
MRS W	Yes, it do, don't it——er, does, doesn't it?
BETH	But now the racing's begun over at Seldon Park things'll buck up, you'll see.
MRS W	I sincerely hope so.
BETH	Oh, arr, and when the summer comes you'll get 'oneymoon couples. I like a nice 'oneymoon, don't you?

Mrs W	I've only experienced one, but it was very pleasant.
Beth	I've had ever so many.
Mrs W	Really?
Beth	Yes, I had three last June, two in July and two more in the autumn.
Mrs W	Goodness me.
Wagstaff	(*coming out of his paper.*) Two 'what' in the autumn?
Beth	'Oneymoons.
Wagstaff	What?
Mrs W	Honeymoons, dear. Beth was telling us about her honeymoons.
Wagstaff	I didn't even know she was married.
Mrs W	No, dear, she means the couples that spend them here.
Wagstaff	Well, I hope we don't have any. Sloppy things——if you ask me.
Mrs W	You had one yourself once.
Wagstaff	I did?——Oh yes, of course, well, that was different.
Beth	I'll 'ave it now.
Mrs W	I beg your pardon?
Beth	The tray.
Wagstaff	I haven't finished yet.
Beth	Proper turn I 'ad in the night. I come over all green and——
Wagstaff	Oh, here, take it.
Beth	Ta. And shivery. That's 'ow my old Granny went out. All green and shivery. Oh, do you want jelly for lunch?
Wagstaff	No!! (Beth *exits.*) If she doesn't leave, I shall.

MRS W	We can't turn her out, Henry, she's got nowhere to go.
WAGSTAFF	I could think of somewhere. I say, Doris, do you regret having taken this place?
MRS W	No, of course not, dear. Why?
WAGSTAFF	Well, it was your idea but, dammit, we are supposed to have retired.
MRS W	I enjoy having something to do, Henry. Besides, we could never have afforded a place like this as a private house.
WAGSTAFF	If we don't get some people here soon we might just as well call it a private house and be done with it.
MRS W	Someone's bound to come soon. You heard Beth say things would pick up.
	(COLONEL WAGSTAFF *turns to go upstairs as* SUSAN *enters through French windows. She is in her early twenties.*)
SUSAN	Good morning, Daddy
WAGSTAFF	Hullo, Susan.
SUSAN	How are you?
WAGSTAFF	Fine, dear, fine.
	(*They kiss.*)
SUSAN	It's beautiful out this morning.
WAGSTAFF	Have you had your breakfast?
SUSAN	Yes, hours ago when you were still snoring.
WAGSTAFF	I——I'll see you later. (WAGSTAFF *exits upstairs.*)
SUSAN	Do you want anything from the village, Mother.
MRS W	Yes, dear, but I'll have to sit down quietly somewhere and make out a list.
SUSAN	Let's do it now, shall we? Here you are. (*Hands her a pad and pencil from table by front door.*)
MRS W	Thank you, dear. Now what do I want?

SUSAN	Salt?
MRS W	Salt.
SUSAN	Pepper?
WAGSTAFF	(*appearing at the head of the stairs.*) Beth!
MRS W	Yes, anything else?
WAGSTAFF	Beth!!
MRS W	Oh, Henry, please be quiet, I'm trying to think.
WAGSTAFF	I'm sorry, dear. (*Puts on a stage whisper.*) Beth.
	(BETH *enters* U.L. *as* COLONEL WAGSTAFF *is calling, and answers, also in a whisper.*)
BETH	Yes, my dear?
WAGSTAFF	Do you happen to have such a thing as a pair of shoe laces about your person?
BETH	Come again.
WAGSTAFF	(*shouting.*) Shoe laces! I want some shoe laces. (*Exits.*)
BETH	I'll go and get some.
MRS W	(*adding to her list.*) Ah, shoe laces.
BETH	(*feeling in her pockets.*) I might have a piece of string on me——I——'ere, what's——oh, a letter. Now where did——oh, aye, I remember, it came yesterday, 'ere you are.
SUSAN	It's addressed to the proprietor.
MRS W	Really, you must be more careful. It might have been important.
BETH	Arr, my stomach put it right out of my head.
WAGSTAFF	(*reappearing.*) Have you got them yet?
MRS W	No, Henry, but there's a letter for you that came yesterday.
WAGSTAFF	Yesterday!
BETH	I'll go and look for them laces! (*Exits in haste with second tray.*)

WAGSTAFF	Who's it from?
SUSAN	Haven't read it yet, but it's a London postmark.
WAGSTAFF	That's a great help.
SUSAN	(*reading.*) 'Dear Sir, I should be most grateful if you could prepare three rooms for next Tuesday. The party will consist of my valet Mr Phipps, my secretary Mr Danby, and myself. Mr Danby, whom I have engaged by post, and who will be joining my staff on Tuesday, will arrive first to see to all arrangements. Yours faithfully, Alfred Tubbe.' Well, that's wonderful.
	(COLONEL *and* MRS WAGSTAFF *both look decidedly nervous.*)
MRS W	How many did he say, dear?
SUSAN	Three in all. He must be very wealthy to afford a staff like that.
WAGSTAFF	Three's rather a lot. It's going to be murder every morning with four people all struggling to get a shave in one bathroom.
SUSAN	You'll have to grow a beard.
WAGSTAFF	Don't be ridiculous. I'm a Colonel, not an Admiral! Anyway, your Mother doesn't like 'em.
SUSAN	I think they're very becoming. (*To her Mother.*) Are you sure you don't like them, Mummy?
MRS W	(*coming out of a reverie.*) What?
SUSAN	Beards.
MRS W	Beards! (*Grabs letter.*) Have they got beards?
SUSAN	Of course not. Daddy was just saying you don't like them.
MRS W	Henry, do stick to the point, and come down off that balcony, you look like Juliet.
WAGSTAFF	(*coming down.*) Juliet who?

Mrs W	(*ignoring him.*) Now, when are they coming?
Susan	On Tuesday.
Wagstaff	Then at least we've got a week to arrange things.
Mrs W	I wish I knew how to begin.
Wagstaff	What's their address?
Susan	181 Grosvenor Terrace, W.1.
Wagstaff	It's a wealthy neighbourhood. In fact I believe my old CO lived there. You remember, dear, Major-General Gladwyn. Nice chap, I lost sight of him when we left Delhi.
Susan	I'm not surprised, it's a long way off.
Mrs W	I do wish you'd concentrate, Henry. I want some constructive ideas as to how we're going to arrange things.
Wagstaff	It was your idea. It's up to you.
Susan	I know, let's ask Beth
Mrs W	Are you being serious?
Susan	She must know how things work here.
Mrs W	I suppose you're right.
Susan	We'll see what she says, anyway——Beth!——It can't do any harm——Beth!
	(*Another crash off-stage.*)
Wagstaff	Can't it?
Mrs W	Well, you'd better keep out of the discussion, dear, you confuse her.
Wagstaff	I do?
	(*Enter* Beth)
Mrs W	Oh, Beth, we've just had a letter from some people asking if they can stay here.
Beth	Oh, 'Ere's your shoe laces, Colonel, my dear.
Wagstaff	Oh, er——thank you.

MRS W	Yes, Beth, the season seems to have begun.
BETH	Aye. I hope you wanted brown.
WAGSTAFF	Yes, they're fine.
BETH	Are they long enough?
MRS W	Beth, will you pay attention to what I'm saying.
BETH	Eh?
MRS W	We have a lot of people arriving.
BETH	When are they coming?
SUSAN	Next Tuesday. Three of them.
BETH	Three, oh well, it won't be a 'oneymoon.
MRS W	Hardly. Now what bedrooms are they going to have?
SUSAN	Well, there's Mr Tubbe, the secretary and valet. Mr Tubbe better have one of those rooms on the landing.
WAGSTAFF	He can't possibly. We use them.
MRS W	We're only using two of them, that's Susan's and our own, the other one's free.
WAGSTAFF	I use it as a dressing room. There are plenty of rooms on the side of the house for visitors.
MRS W	Beth, how do the guests usually sleep here?
BETH	Oh, not bad. Some complain about the ——
MRS W	I mean where do they sleep? In those rooms (*pointing to top of stairs*) or the ones at the side?
BETH	Those.
MRS W	There, Henry, I thought so. You'll just have to sacrifice a little space.
WAGSTAFF	I'm damned if I do. I bought this place because I wanted to live in pleasant surroundings, not a second-rate boarding house.
MRS W	Right, well, that's fixed.
WAGSTAFF	Look here, Doris, I do not intend to have my privacy violated by trippers.

Mrs W	Who said anything about trippers?
Wagstaff	I have a horror of people who come pouring through the door with packets of greasy sandwiches and buckets and spades.
Mrs W	We happen to be in the heart of the country, dear.
	(*There is a knock at the door.*)
	Beth, see who that is.
Wagstaff	I don't care where we are, I don't like them, and if anyone like that dares to come here, they can go straight out again. You understand? Straight out!
	(Beth *opens the door and* John Danby *enters. He's an engaging young man of about twenty-five, dapper and very 'public school.'*)
Beth	Er——Colonel Wagstaff, sir, there's a —
Wagstaff	(*with his back to the door and ignoring everything.*) Don't interrupt. I'm talking. And as for those rooms up there (*pointing dramatically*), they constitute my castle——
Mrs W	Darling——
Wagstaff	A castle which I've been dreaming of and carefully planning all my life. (Mrs Wagstaff *signals* Danby *to sit down and smiles graciously*). I am king of that castle and you can take it from me there'll be no dirty rascals.
Susan	(*to* Danby). Won't you sit down?
Wagstaff	No, I won't sit down!
Danby	No, thank you.
Wagstaff	And if anyone——. What is going on? Beth, I told you——. (*Sees* Danby.) Oh, er——how do you do?
Danby	Good morning.
Wagstaff	I don't think I know you, do I?

DANBY	No, my name is Danby.
WAGSTAFF	Mine's Wagstaff, Colonel Wagstaff.
	(*They shake hands.*)
DANBY	How do you do?
WAGSTAFF	Darling, this is my wife. (*Points to* DANBY) I mean this is my wife. Doris, this is Mr Dagby.
DANBY	Danby.
WAGSTAFF	Danby.
DANBY	How do you do?
SUSAN	(*aghast*). Danby?
MRS W	Susan, really!
SUSAN	You must be the person mentioned in this letter.
DANBY	Must I?
SUSAN	Mother, this is Mr Danby who's arriving on Tuesday.
MRS W	All right, dear, well, I——
SUSAN	To-day is Tuesday!?
MRS W	Yes, but they're coming next——. Oh dear, you are coming next Tuesday, aren't you?
DANBY	Why, is it someone's birthday?
MRS W	No, no, but——but Mr——er——Tubbe didn't mean today, did he?
DANBY	I hope he did.
MRS W	Oh.
DANBY	May I see the letter?
MRS W	Yes, certainly. (*Gives it to him.*)
DANBY	It was posted on Saturday, he obviously thought you'd get it on Monday.
BETH	Oh, aye, it came on Monday and I——(*realizes she's put her foot in it*)——I'll go and see about summat. (*Exits.*)

WAGSTAFF	There you have the cause of the trouble, Mr Dombey.
MRS W	Digby.
WAGSTAFF	Digby.
SUSAN	Danby.
WAGSTAFF	Danby.
DANBY	Sounds like a train, diddle-ee-dom-diddle-ee-dy-diddle-ee-dom. Yes, well, if you are booked up already, I'd better——
MRS W	Oh good heavens no, we have no one here at all——(*quickly*) at the moment. We'd be delighted to accommodate you, wouldn't we, Henry.
WAGSTAFF	Delighted, yes, delighted.
SUSAN	Where's the rest of your party, they're not outside, are they?
DANBY	No. I came on to make sure everything was ready for Mr Tubbe. I'm his secretary, or rather will be. I haven't met him yet.
MRS W	Which room do you suppose he'd like?
DANBY	The best one, I should think.
MRS W	Susan, would you show Mr Danby the dressing room.
SUSAN	Yes, I'd love to.
MRS W	I think he'll find it very comfortable.
DANBY	Are you sure it's all right? I gather the Colonel was rather keen on using it.
MRS W	Nonsense, you never go near it, do you, Henry? (COLONEL WAGSTAFF *is about to reply.*) No, I thought not. Go along, dear. (*To* SUSAN.)
SUSAN	Right. I'll lead the way. Oh, and keep in the middle of the stairs as much as possible.
DANBY	Why?

SUSAN	There's a spot of dry rot along the edge. (DANBY *jumps smartly into the middle.*)
DANBY	Lead on, MacDuff. (*They start off upstairs.* SUSAN *stops.*)
SUSAN	Lay on.
DANBY	I beg your pardon.
SUSAN	It's 'Lay on, MacDuff.'
DANBY	Oh, I see. (*They get to the top of the stairs.*)
SUSAN	I'm sorry, It's not very polite to correct a perfect stranger.
DANBY	Oh, we can soon put that right. My name is John Danby and yours is Susan Wagstaff. Right?
SUSAN	Right.
DANBY	I'm delighted to meet you, Miss Wagstaff. (*Shakes her hand.*)
SUSAN	Thank you, Mr Danby.
DANBY	Not at all. Lead——er, lay on, Miss Wagstaff. (*They exit.*)
WAGSTAFF	Mad, you see. I'm surrounded by lunatics.
MRS W	Henry.
WAGSTAFF	Two upstairs, one drooling around in the kitchen, and probably a couple more by now sitting on the doorstep.
MRS W	(*looking upstairs*). I think he's very charming. I'm sure they'll make ideal visitors.
WAGSTAFF	Why do they have to take our rooms? I——
MRS W	Now listen, I don't want to hear another word about it.
WAGSTAFF	Very well, but don't blame me when you find yourself sleeping on the sofa.
MRS W	No dear, I won't. Now, if you don't mind I'll ask Beth to get the room ready.

WAGSTAFF	If she's going to be let loose, I'm going out to do some gardening.
MRS W	Very good idea. Oh, you might bring in some flowers, they'll liven the place up a bit.
WAGSTAFF	Wouldn't like a small orchestra, would you? (*Exits through French windows,* R.)
MRS W	Beth!
	(DANBY *and* SUSAN *enter upstairs.*)
DANBY	It's a charming room, Mrs Wagstaff. That'll do splendidly.
MRS W	Good.
BETH	Did you call me? (*Entering.*)
MRS W	Yes, I did. Will you collect all Colonel Wagstaff's things from his dressing-room and put them into our room.
BETH	He won't blame I, will he?
MRS W	Oh, stop asking silly questions and get on with it.
BETH	(*resigned.*) Arr. (*Exit upstairs.*)
SUSAN	Is there anything I can be doing?
MRS W	Not at the moment, dear.
SUSAN	Don't forget there's still the shopping. Daddy could take me in the car.
MRS W	Well, he's gardening now.
· DANBY	Can't you ask him to stop gardening?
MRS W	Well, it's not really advisable.
SUSAN	Let me drive it in, I'm pretty good now, all I need is practice.
MRS W	No, dear, that's even less advisable.
DANBY	Well, if it's any help, I have a car outside.
MRS W	Oh I wouldn't dream of troubling you.
DANBY	It's no trouble at all.

Mrs W	(*easily won*). Splendid. Susan, where's that list I was making?
Susan	It's here.
Mrs W	Don't forget to take it with you.
Susan	This won't go far with seven people in the house. Salt and pepper.
Mrs W	Isn't there something else?
Susan	(*looks at list*). Shoe laces.
Mrs W	Ah, yes, I thought so. (*Exits* D.L.)
Danby	My arrival seems to have caused a minor earthquake.
	(Beth *is heard knocking things about.*)
	Do you have this sort of upheaval every time someone comes?
Susan	Well, I'll be perfectly honest with you, if you promise not to breathe a word to the other guests.
Danby	Secrets?
Susan	Just a little one.
Danby	I promise.
Susan	You're the first people we've had since we bought the place.
Danby	(*laughing*). Oh, I see.
Susan	It's no joke, believe me, it's nerve-wracking.
	(Beth *drops another heavy object upstairs and a shout is heard.*)
Danby	Yes, I see what you mean.
Susan	That's Beth.
Danby	So I gathered.
Susan	She's not really as bad as she seems.
Danby	I am relieved to hear it.

SUSAN	She was in the place when we bought it.
DANBY	That must have brought the price down quite a lot. Do you live here?
SUSAN	Yes. I was going to be a secretary, but I thought I could be more useful here than pushing a pen in some dreary office.
DANBY	You obviously haven't got a very high opinion of secretaries.
SUSAN	No. Oh, I'm sorry, I forgot. Perhaps we'd better go before I say anything else wrong.
DANBY	Right. (*Opens front door.*) Let's shop down and do the popping——er——pop down and do the shopping.
	(*They exit.*)
	(BETH *comes to the head of the stairs with a suitcase and calls:*)
BETH	Colonel Wagstaff, Colonel Wagstaff! Oh heck! (*She receives no answer and starts walking downstairs with case.*) Colonel Wagstaff!
	(COLONEL WAGSTAFF *comes in through the French windows.*)
WAGSTAFF	(*seeing* BETH *with the case*). Will you be away long?
BETH	Eh? No, I'm looking for you.
WAGSTAFF	Are you eloping?
BETH	No, I've been having trouble with your drawers.
WAGSTAFF	I beg your pardon!
BETH	They were stuck. I couldn't budge 'em.
WAGSTAFF	Oh, I'm not surprised. There happens to be a key. (*Handing her the key.*)
BETH	No, I've done it now. It weren't 'arf a proper struggle.
WAGSTAFF	But there's a lock on them.

BETH	Was there? Well, there isn't now.
	(*Phone rings.*)
WAGSTAFF	You clumsy fool! (*Rushes upstairs to inspect the damage and ignores the phone.*)
BETH	Oh 'eck. (*Lifts up receiver and holds it with mouthpiece at eye-level.*) Yes, 'ullo. I'm very well, thanks, how are you?——What? Oh, I thought you said 'How am I?'——I'm Beth, B-E-T——Eh? — Who's drunk? Oh, trunks. 'Ang on. (COLONEL WAGSTAFF *comes downstairs.*) It's Trunks, Colonel——'ang on——hurry up, my dear——just coming——'ere we are.
	(COLONEL WAGSTAFF *takes phone.*)
WAGSTAFF	Hullo, yes, speaking——What's that? Oh yes, we're quite close to the racecourse here——Oh ——a room for a jockey on Friday? Hold on ——Doris!
MRS W	(*off.*) Yes?
WAGSTAFF	Would you care for a jockey next Friday?
MRS W	(*enters.*) What, dear? (*She comes on with a 'Register.'*)
WAGSTAFF	A jockey, dear. Have we room for one on Friday?
MRS W	I should think so. They're quite small.
WAGSTAFF	Well, I don't know whether——
MRS W	Of course we have room for him.
WAGSTAFF	(*into phone.*) Yes, we can do it then.
MRS W	And his horse.
WAGSTAFF	And his horse——What? Oh yes, of course. (*To* DORIS.) Don't be silly, dear. (*Back to phone.*) Yes, all right——thank you. Good-bye.
MRS W	Well, this is splendid, we shall be full before we know where we are.
WAGSTAFF	I see nothing splendid about it. I sense an impending disaster. I'm going back to the garden. I was in the middle of digging a trench.

Mrs W	What for, celery?
Wagstaff	No, a siege! (*Exits.*)
Mrs W	Have you finished upstairs yet?
Beth	No.
Mrs W	Well, do hurry, please. Then just clear around in here.
Beth	I'll 'ave a proper bash at it, eh?
Mrs W	Well, just a gentle tap would do.
Beth	All right.

(*Goes clumping back upstairs knocking paint off everything with the case and* Mrs Wagstaff *goes back into the kitchen.*)

(*There's a knock on the door. But no one answers it.*)

Fred	(*off.*) No answer, guv.
Alf	(*off.*) Why don't you push the perishing bell?
Fred	I 'ave, it don't work.
Alf	Knock then.
Fred	(*knocks again.*) That didn't work either.
Alf	Well, kick it. I can't stand 'ere all day.
Fred	All right.

(Mrs Wagstaff *comes on to open the door, just as* Fred *has raised his leg to kick and it shoots out in front of him and he collapses into the room.* Alfred Tubbe *is a large man of the bookmaking fraternity. He always wears, or carries, throughout the entire play a black homberg hat. He's about fifty and* Frederick Phipps *is his runner, a North Country man. A bit dim but very likeable.*)

Alf	(*immediately putting on a posh voice.*) How do you do, dear lady?
Mrs W	How do you do.
Alf	Alfred Tubbe is my name and this is my valet, Frederick Phipps.

MRS W	Really.
	(MRS WAGSTAFF *is looking down at* FRED, *who is still on the floor.*)
ALF	Off your knees, Frederick.
	(FRED *gets up.*)
	I believe my secretary will be here waiting for me.
MRS W	Oh yes, a Mr Danby.
FRED	That's the geezer!
ALF	(*trying to muzzle him with his hand.*) Easy, lad!——Er——Yes, Danby's the name. I engaged him by post and arranged for him to join my little entourage here.
FRED	Eh? (*Not understanding, his mouth wide open.*)
ALF	(*quietly.*) Shut your mouth, boy.
MRS W	I believe he's out at the moment, but do come in, won't you?
ALF	Thanks. Ah, ah, one of the stately homes of old England. It's got class. Très distingué as we say on the Riviera.
MRS W	Oh, you've been to France?
FRED	No, the Riviera.
	(ALF *freezes him with a look.*)
ALF	Bit of a wag, isn't he? Don't wag too far, Phipps, or you might fall over.
MRS W	I've always wanted to go to France. Do you speak French?
ALF	(*on his guard.*) Oh well—er—you know—Do you?
MRS W	No, not a word. Do you?
ALF	(*relieved.*) Fluidly.
MRS W	My husband and I have spent most of our lives in India.

ALF	Oh hot, very hot——yes.
MRS W	Er—yes—well if you'll excuse me I must go and see to things in the kitchen. Just ring if you want anything.
ALF	Thank you.
	(MRS WAGSTAFF *exits*.)
FRED	'Ere, what's the idea of all this lah-di-dah?
ALF	Now look, Fred, you remember what 'appened last time we tried to switch racehorses.
FRED	Aye.
ALF	What?
FRED	Police nearly nabbed us.
ALF	But why?
FRED	You couldn't run fast enough.
ALF	No!!
FRED	I give up.
ALF	Because we looked suspicious and mixed with the crooks and the riff-raff. They'd have said 'Guilty' before we'd even had a trial. Just by the company we kept.
FRED	It's not right, is it, it's not fair.
ALF	No, and they calls it Justice. It's getting so a crook daren't show his face in daylight.
FRED	Aye.
ALF	And the law's cutting its own throat with this persecution. They're driving us underground!
FRED	Aye.
ALF	And they'll never find us, it's a hopeless situation. I see nothing but disaster for the country.
FRED	Aye.
ALF	Now take me for instance. A respectable bookie with a valet and a secretary; who'd accuse me of switching racehorses?

FRED	(*brightly*.) Police?
ALF	(*nods*.) Police——. (*Quickly*.) No! No one. But on Saturday we're going to do the biggest switch we ever done. Kidnap the favourite, Cardinal, when it's flown over from France, and substitute Sweet Lavender, who can just about stand.
FRED	Aye, but what about the French stable lad travelling wit' Cardinal, he'll wonder what's up.
ALF	He's been squared.
FRED	Oh.
ALF	Now, with Sweet Lavender running for the Cardinal, Cardinal loses.
FRED	What's the good of that?
ALF	I've backed it to lose.
FRED	Why?
ALF	I get better odds that way.
FRED	'Ow much are we going to make?
ALF	Only a cool ten thousand.
FRED	Oh, only a cool ten——(*Doubletakes*)——ten thousand!!
ALF	We shove in Sweet Lavender, it loses, and we get ten thousand pounds for our troubles.
FRED	Sounds easy when you put it like that.
ALF	Course it's easy.
FRED	Well, where are we going to hide all these flipping horses?
ALF	Now stop worrying. Flash Harry's seeing to all that. I've wired him to meet us here this morning, he'll give us all the dope.
FRED	Good.
ALF	In the meantime remember we've got to look inconspicuous. I'm a respectable gentleman with a secretary.

FRED	Is that why I have to be your valet instead of your 'runner'?
ALF	Valay, Fred, I keep telling you 'valay' like in Wales.
FRED	Wales?
ALF	Rhondda Valley!
FRED	Oh aye. Rhondda Valley. I'll remember.
ALF	Well, see you do.
FRED	'Ere what about this secretary bloke? You'll 'ave to square him before he puts his foot in it.
ALF	Don't be stupid, he might not play; I'm going to fool him same as the others.
FRED	It's a risk, guv.
ALF	Not if you don't let me down. That's why I've engaged him, to keep things classy even if you make a mess of it all.
FRED	Well, I like that!
ALF	I'm glad to hear it.
	(*There is a knock at the door.*)
	Ssh!
FRED	What's up?
	(MRS WAGSTAFF *comes in to answer the door.*)
ALF	(*to* MRS WAGSTAFF.) Someone is without!
	(FRED, *not understanding, thinks* ALF *is referring to his trousers and looks down to make sure they are on.* MRS WAGSTAFF *opens the door and reveals* FLASH HARRY. *He is a crook with a flow of talk.*)
FLASH	Hullo, Mr Tubbe 'ere yet? Eh? Is he 'er yet, is he? Mr Tubbe? Eh? Is he 'ere?
MRS W	Mr Tubbe?
FLASH	Yes, Mr Tubbe, that's right, is he 'ere yet?
MRS W	Yes. Won't you come in?

FLASH	Ta, thanks, ta very much. (*Sees* ALF *and* FRED.) Hullo, Freddie boy, Alf you old barrel you!
FRED	(*assuming his roll of valet for* MRS WAGSTAFF'S *sake.*) Was you referring to the master?
FLASH	Eh? (FRED *knocks on* ALF'S *hat.*)
ALF	Come in!
FRED	Please, Mr Tubbe there's a Mr Flash Harry to see you.
FLASH	'Ere, what kind of a caper...
ALF	(*seizing him quickly by the hand.*) How d'you do. Pleased to see you, Flash. Of course you remember my 'valet' Mr Phipps, don't you?
FLASH	No. (ALF *twists his hand.*) Yes!!
ALF	Yes, I thought you would and this is the good lady of the house, Mrs Wagstaff. (*introduces her.*) Mr Flash Harold.
FLASH	(*looking baffled.*) 'Ow do.
MRS W	How do you do? Well, if you'll excuse me——
ALF	Certainly. If you've gotter go, you've gotter go.
MRS W	I'll tell Beth to collect your things.
ALF	Thank you, no hurry, any time will suffice.
	(MRS WAGSTAFF *exits.*)
FLASH	Suffice! Suffice?
FRED	Ssh!!
FLASH	(*points to* ALF.) Where's 'e been? Night school?
ALF	We're laying it on a bit posh, see.
FLASH	I should say you was. What's the idea eh, I've never——
ALF	Listen.
FLASH	Yeah, I'm listening; cor, what a carry on. 'How-d'you-flippin'-do' she says. (*Minces round.*)
ALF	Listen!

FLASH	Let me 'intro-blooming-duce' you to the lady of the house.
FRED	Ssh!
FLASH	That'll suf-flippin'-fice!
ALF	Your face'll flippin' suffer if you don't shut up!
FLASH	Well——
ALF	I'm down 'ere as a high-class bookie.
FRED	And I'm his valise.
ALF	A right case you are! And I'm 'aving a secretary to add a spot of class so don't put your foot in it. We don't want the police around.
FRED	Aye, we've got to be 'inconspicuous.'
FLASH	Cor, lie down, lad, and have a glass of water.
ALF	What's the news of Sweet Lavender?
FLASH	Its 'ere.
ALF	Where?
FLASH	In the field. (*Points through window.*)
ALF ⎫ FRED ⎭	In the field!
FLASH	Now simmer down. It's all right.
ALF	(*about to explode.*) You b——
FLASH	Listen! Don't be so 'eadstrong, Alfred, you're shocking the servants. (*Points to* FRED.)
ALF	I'll shock you if you don't——
FLASH	Look. (*Points through windows.*) You see that clump of trees?
ALF	Yes.
FLASH	In the middle of that there's an old convent.
ALF	What about the nuns?
FLASH	There ain't none. It's a ruin. Now in the middle of the ruin there's a barn.

ALF	We can't risk 'aving it in a barn!
FLASH	Wait, I 'aven't finished yet. Now inside the barn the floor comes up.
ALF	Eh?
FLASH	Where's me glass of water?
ALF	Quiet!
FLASH	There's two big trapdoors and some sort of steps lead down to a sort of cellar.
ALF	What is it?
FLASH	Sort of cellar, it's got all sorts of passages and things, but it makes a lovely stable.
ALF	'Ave you got Sweet Lavender there now?
FLASH	Yeah, snug as a bug, and you'll be able to keep an eye on it from 'ere like.
ALF	Yes.
FLASH	Then when the Cardinal arrives in the country I'll collect it from the airport, drive it down 'ere, dump it, pick up dear old Sweet Lavender and take it to the course, and Bob's your uncle.
ALF	You're making sure Sweet Lavender's too weak to win?
FLASH	Weak! He's had so many sleeping pills every time we hang his nose-bag on he falls flat on his face.
ALF	Right, well scapa now and mind how you go.
FLASH	OK, Alfie boy.
MRS W	(*off.*) Beth!
	(*Enter* MRS WAGSTAFF.)
ALF	(*hurriedly.*) Look out. (*They all remove their hats.*)
MRS W	Has Beth come down yet?
ALF	I fear not.
MRS W	Oh dear.

ALF	Well good-bye, Harold.
FLASH	(*in a plummy voice.*) Toodle-pip, Alfred. (*To* FRED) Good-bye, my man.
	(FRED *opens the front door for* HARRY.)
FRED	G'bye, Mr Flash, sir. (*Holds out his hand.*) I trust as 'ow you've been comfortable.
FRED	(*tipping him.*) Only half a crown but I hope it'll suffice!
	(*Winks at* ALF *and walks into door-post.*)
	(*Exits.*)
	(MRS WAGSTAFF *goes back to kitchen calling for* BETH *Exits.*)
ALF	Phew, let's have that drink, boy.
FRED	No one serving.
ALF	Ring the bell then.
FRED	Where is it?
ALF	Must be one by the bar.
FRED	(*goes down* L. *to a beam.*) This looks like it. (*Pushes and nothing happens.*) (*Whispering.*) Did you 'ear anything?
ALF	(*taking* FRED'S *tone.*) No, what?
FRED	I didn't either.
ALF	What the 'ell are you talking about?
FRED	The bell, it don't work.
ALF	Don't any of the bells 'ere work?
FRED	Shall I kick this one, too?
ALF	Yes, might as well. (*Not really taking much notice.*)
FRED	Righto.
	(*He does so. And as he kicks it a panel in the back wall flies open.*)
ALF	Take it easy, you'll 'ave the wall down.

FRED	(*turning, sees the open panel.*) Ee, guv, look, I 'ave!!
ALF	Yes, so I should think. (*Turns and then doubletakes.*) 'Struth! 'Ere, what 'ave you done?
FRED	I never done anything. I never went near it.
ALF	Well, you must have kicked something that worked it.
FRED	No, I only kicked the bell like that. (*Does so and the panel shuts.*) And I'll cripple myself if I do it again.
ALF	Yes, but there must——
FRED	'Ere, it's shut.
ALF	Blimey. 'Ere, let's 'ave a butchers'. It must be this notch here, it's a bit out of line with the others, see?
FRED	Can you move it with your hands?
ALF	No, it needs force.
FRED	I wonder if they know about it.
ALF	I don't know. Now listen, Fred, don't let on about it. I'll test the ground a bit first, see. Use a little diplomacy.
FRED	Use what?
ALF	Me nut.
FRED	Oh aye.
ALF	I'll bring the conversation round subtle like and then when I ask them sort of airily if there's a secret panel in the house, watch 'em and see if there's any sort of glances before they answer.
FRED	Ok.'Ere, what you say we 'ave another look, eh? Just to make sure it is that brick and not someone 'aving a lark with us?
ALF	'Ow d'yer mean?
FRED	(*gets softer and softer during this speech in case they're being spied on.*) Well there might be a bloke with his eyes on us without us knowing. He may

have thought there was no one here and opened the panel just when I 'appened to kick the brick. Then seeing us 'ere, covers up by making us think that we're working it.

ALF   (*straining to hear.*) 'Aven't been sitting in a draught, have you?

FRED   Ssh!!

ALF   What's up?

FRED   He may be watching us. Now then, how are we going to kick that notch again without him knowing and working it like he did before?

ALF   You better take it by surprise.

FRED   That's it. I'll sneak up on it. We'll just act casual like——don't let on. (*Starts to whistle and amble round.*)

ALF   (*humming.*) Been reading much lately?

FRED   Hoffanon.

ALF   Who's it by?

FRED   Yes.

ALF   Oh.

       (FRED *makes as though to kick but then whips round to see if panel is open.*)

       You missed it.

FRED   I was just pretending, thought I might catch him, see?

ALF   Never mind that, get a move on——someone may come in.

FRED   OK, guv.

       (*Whistling and ambling business repeated.* COLONEL WAGSTAFF *enters unseen and stares in amazement.* FRED, *who is pirouetting, sees him and freezes.* ALF *sees nothing and continues humming.*)

       (*to* COLONEL WAGSTAFF.) How d'you do, guv'nor?

ALF	How d'you do.
WAGSTAFF	How do you do.
ALF	Ah echo.
FRED	(*trying to attract* ALF'S *attention.*) How d'you do.
ALF	Not again. (*Turns and sees* WAGSTAFF. *Rises and puts on his posh voice again.*) How do you do, sir?
WAGSTAFF	I'm very well, thank you.
ALF	Good.
WAGSTAFF	May I ask what you're doing here?
ALF	We're guests. My name is Alfred Tubbe.
WAGSTAFF	My God, is it? I mean——really, oh mine's Wagstaff.
ALF	Pleased to meet you, I'm sure. (*Shakes hands.*) This is Mr Frederick Phipps.
WAGSTAFF	Oh. (*Shakes hands.*)
FRED	That's right. I'm Mr Tubbe's Cardiff.
ALF	(*quickly.*) Rhondda!
FRED	Rhondda. Valley! Yes, valley.
ALF	Bit of a humourist at times.
WAGSTAFF	Really? Well, if you'll excuse me, I've been digging in the garden. I'm looking for my wife.
FRED	Is she dead? (*Removes his cap.*)
	(ALF *kicks him.*)
WAGSTAFF	What?
ALF	Ah, your wife. I suppose that was the very charming lady we met when we arrived.
WAGSTAFF	Yes, I suppose it was.
ALF	We were having quite a pleasant chat until duty called.
WAGSTAFF	Oh, have you seen your rooms yet?
ALF	No, not yet.

WAGSTAFF	Well, I'll get your things taken up. (*Calls.*) Beth! Your secretary was here earlier this morning and, er, 'chose' your room. I trust you'll find it all right.
FRED	Why, is it far?
ALF	Phipps, go and get the luggage out of the car.
FRED	Okey dokey. (*Exits.*)
WAGSTAFF	Beth!!——Might as well talk to myself. It's like this from morning till night. Beth!!
	(*Enter* MRS WAGSTAFF.)
MRS W	Oh, do stop shouting, Henry, I can't hear myself cook.
WAGSTAFF	Well, where the devil's Beth got to?
MRS W	Upstairs, and if you must shout do it quietly.
WAGSTAFF	(*cooing.*) Beth.
	(BETH *emerges at head of stairs.*)
BETH	Yes, my dear?
MRS W	(*to* HENRY.) There, you see! Have you finished the room?
BETH	Arr, you wouldn't recognize it now.
WAGSTAFF	So I can imagine. Go and give a hand with some luggage, will you?
BETH	Yes, me dear. (*Comes downstairs and notices* ALF.) 'Ullo, me dear.
ALF	'Ow do, ducks. (*Realizes his slip.*)
	(BETH *reaches door as* FRED *enters with two suitcases. It is love at first sight.* BETH *and* FRED *melt at the sight of each other.*)
BETH	Oh, good morning. Can I have your name, please?
FRED	Fred Phipps. What's yours?
BETH	Beth Barton.

FRED	Beg pardon?
BETH	No. Beth Barton.
FRED	Oh. (*Giggles.*) 'Ullo.
MRS W	Beth!
BETH	Oh. 'Ere's another visitor. (*Introduces them.*) Mr Phipps——Colonel Wagstaff.
MRS W	They already know each other.
BETH	Small world, isn't it?
WAGSTAFF	It'll be smaller still if you don't bring that luggage in. (BETH *exits.*)
MRS W	(*pouring oil.*) Let me show you your room, Mr Tubbe.
ALF	Of course, dear lady.
	(*They go upstairs.*)
MRS W	Oh, by the way, keep to the centre of the stairs, there's a spot of dry rot coming up the side.
FRED	(*thinking she means him.*) Eh?
ALF	Not you, the woodwork.
MRS W	I do hope you like it. It's a charming room, and it's got Wedgwood and Chippendale in it.
FRED	Ee, there'll be quite a crowd of you!
ALF	Chippendale refers to the furniture.
FRED	What does Wedgwood refer to?
MRS W	The pottery.
	(ALF *and* FRED *stare at each other and* ALF *claps his hand over* FRED'S *mouth before he can speak. Exeunt.* WAGSTAFF *looks utterly bewildered and goes to the bar down* L. *and pours himself a drink.* BETH *enters with two more cases. One has* 'HONEST ALF' *written on it.*)
BETH	Where shall I put these?
WAGSTAFF	You can put them upstairs with the others.
	(SUSAN *and* DANBY *enter with suitcases.*)

(BETH *exits upstairs.*)

SUSAN	Hullo, Daddy, whose is the car outside?
WAGSTAFF	Mr Danby's future employer.
DANBY	Mr Tubbe? Oh, what's he like?
WAGSTAFF	Large.
DANBY	How does he strike you?
WAGSTAFF	I'm hoping things will look better through a haze of alcohol. Have one?
DANBY	No thanks. You know, I'm beginning to wonder if I'm going to enjoy my new career.
WAGSTAFF	I know exactly how you feel.
BETH	(*off.*) Yes, Mr Tubbe, thank you, Mr Tubbe. (*She comes whistling downstairs.*)
SUSAN	Beth seems pleased with everything.
BETH	'Eere, look, ten bob just for taking his cases up.
DANBY	Good Lord, are there any more?
BETH	No.
DANBY	Oh well, I'll bring them down when we go!

(MRS WAGSTAFF *at head of stairs sees* MR DANBY *and calls to* ALF.)

MRS W	Oh, Mr Tubbe, Mr Danby's downstairs.

(MR TUBBE *enters, with* FRED *following.*)

ALF	Oh, tophole. I'm delighted to welcome you to my staff, young man. I trust you'll be very 'appy here.
DANBY	Thank you, sir.

(DANBY *is standing next to* SUSAN *and has his case in his hand.*)

ALF	(*seeing* SUSAN *next to* DANBY) You didn't tell me you were married.
DANBY	Married?

ALF	Who is this young lady then?
SUSAN	Oh, I'm not his wife.
ALF	Oh you devils you!
SUSAN	Mr Tubbe, I live here, this is my home.
ALF	Oh, then you're not——?
SUSAN	No, I'm not!
ALF	Pardon my clanger. Delighted to meet you, Miss Wagstaff.
SUSAN	How do you do?
ALF	And this is my valet, Mr Phipps. (*Points to* FRED)
FRED	Pleased to meet you. (*Shakes* ALF's *hand.*)
	(ALF *pulls his hand away.*)
ALF	Now, what about a drink, eh?
WAGSTAFF	No thanks, just had one.
ALF	And charge them all up to me.
WAGSTAFF	Well, perhaps just a small one. Beth, see to them, will you?
FRED	(*to* BETH.) Let me do it for you, can I?
BETH	All right.
FRED	Ta.
	(*From now on,* FRED *is pouring drinks and handing them round ad lib.*)
ALF	Well, Danby, I hope you've come prepared to work. Bookmaking is a full-time job. You'll have plenty to do in a vast organization like mine dealing with large sums of money. I think I can safely say large sums, eh Frederick?
FRED	Eh? Oh aye, hundreds.
ALF	Thousands.
FRED	Hundreds and thousands.
MRS W	Oh, that reminds me. I must see to the trifle. (FRED *is offering her a drink.*) No thank you. (*exits.*)

(FRED *doesn't give it to someone else, but knocks it back and goes to pour another one.*)

ALF
Come to Alfred Tubbe, the biggest bookie in the business.

DANBY
Actually, I don't know an awful lot about it.

ALF
You only want a quick brain for fiddling figures. You'll soon pick it up.

DANBY
Maths was never my strong point at school.

ALF
Where were you at school?

DANBY
Harrow.

ALF
Same 'ere. Whereabouts in 'Arrow?

DANBY
Oh, very good. (*Laughs*)

(ALF *looks blankly.*)

FRED
(*handing drink to* SUSAN.) 'Ere.

SUSAN
Not for me. I must help mother. Come along, Beth. (*She exits.*)

(BETH *waves good-bye to* FRED *who waves back.*)

(BETH *exits and* FRED *gulps down the drink in his hand.*)

ALF
This is a delightful mansion, Mr Wagstaff, I bet you were mad to have it.

WAGSTAFF
I'm beginning to think so.

ALF
Tell me, is it very old? It looks quite historical, doesn't it, Fred?

(FRED *hiccoughs.*)

WAGSTAFF
It's about three hundred years old, I think.

FRED
(*to* DANBY.) 'Ere you are.

DANBY
No thanks, not just now.

FRED
Oh. (*Knocks it back and staggers back to the bar for another one.*)

ALF
Any ghosts or strange things about the place?

WAGSTAFF	Only the maid.
DANBY	It's probably riddled with secret panels.
ALF	That'll do!
DANBY	What?
ALF	(*recovering himself.*) I mean that'll do, Fred, no more.
	(FRED *knocks back the drink he has in his hand and sinks onto his knees behind the bar, unnoticed.*)
DANBY	Well, if you'll excuse me, I'll go and unpack.
ALF	Don't be long.
DANBY	No. Oh, which is my room?
WAGSTAFF	I'll lead the way, some of these passages are a bit confusing. (*Goes upstairs.*) Oh, and keep in the middle.
DANBY	(*following him.*) I know——dry rot.
WAGSTAFF	If you want anything, Mr Tubbe, just ring the bell.
ALF	That one? (*Pointing to the beam* D.L.)
WAGSTAFF	Yes.
ALF	It doesn't work. I've tried it.
WAGSTAFF	The bells are always going on the blink, better try kicking it.
ALF	We did——er——I mean if we did, would anything happen?
WAGSTAFF	Nothing, except perhaps a hole in the wall. Come along. (*To Danby.*)
	(*Exeunt.* FRED *meanwhile has got to his feet and has poured out another drink, in his stupor he puts the glass on the shelf and brings the bottle over.*)
FRED	'Aveadrinkmistubbe.
ALF	(*preoccupied with what* WAGSTAFF *has said.*) No, you have one for a change.

FRED	Thankseversomuch. (*Applies himself to the bottle and falls down behind the bar.*)
	(ALF *is inspecting the panelling as* FLASH HARRY *enters from front door.*)
FLASH	Alf!
ALF	(*startled.*) Eh!
FLASH	Got a torch?
ALF	What for?
FLASH	I've lost Sweet Lavender.
ALF	Lost 'im?
FLASH	Yeah. Well it's so dark in that cellar I can't find him.
ALF	Can't have got out, can he?
FLASH	'Course not. He's in there somewhere.
ALF	We'll have a look in a minute. Now I've got something to tell you. I've found a secret panel.
FLASH	What? Let's have a look! Where's Fred?
ALF	In the kitchen I should think, chasing the maid. See that notch? Watch! (*Kicks notch and panel opens.*)
	(FRED *is now getting to his feet by the panel, he leans on it and disappears through it as it opens.*)
FLASH	Nothin's happened. (*Sees panel.*) Blimey! It's dark, ain't it? (*Sniffs.*) Funny smell.
ALF	Yus.
FLASH	Let's go in.
ALF	OK (*They are just going in when* ALF *stops.*) Wait, did you 'ear anything?
	(*Horse neigh.* FRED *comes running out of panel clutching his backside.*)
FRED	It's Sweet Lavender!!
	(FLASH *and* ALF *dive into panel.* FRED *runs D.L. and kicks notch. The panel closes.* FRED *falls flat on his face, as the curtain falls.*)

Scene Two

It is morning, three days later.

> ALF *puts his head through dining-room door, sees the stage is empty and beckons* FRED *to follow. They both come out stealthily.*

ALF   Come on, it's all right, and bring the grub for Flash.

FRED   Aye. (*He brings an attache case filled with sandwiches and a flask. He trips and almost falls.*)

ALF   Sh! Give it 'ere before you spread it on the wall! 'Urry up and open the panel. Flash'll be hungry guarding that horse all night.

FRED   Why can't he go out for his meals?

ALF   There's no point in him risking being seen when we can keep him supplied through 'ere.

FRED   Well, I'm fed up with you taking all my grub to feed him. Since Tuesday all I've had is rice pudding and semolina.

ALF   It's good for you, ain't it?

FRED   I've only had that 'cos you can't stuff it in your pocket.

ALF   Look, you can't expect to make ten thousand pounds without some 'ardship. You want jam on it, don't you?

FRED   Aye, it might give it a bit of taste.

ALF   Oh shut up. Kick it open.

> (BETH *enters with broom and duster.*)

BETH   Morning, my dears!

> (ALF *closes the case quickly and* FRED, *who has taken a hefty kick, checks himself and does a little dance step.*)

ALF   One, two, three. One, two, three. Oh, that's coming on nicely, Fred you'll be able to go to the ball after all!

BETH	You going to a ball, Fred?
FRED	Eh? Oh—er—aye.
BETH	(*ogling him.*) I can dance, too, Fred.
FRED	(*by now quite smitten.*) Can you?
BETH	Arr.
FRED	Oh.
BETH	Arr.
FRED	Ee.
ALF	(*in disgust.*) Ugh! (*Exits to dining-room.*)
BETH	I like ee.
FRED	Do you?
BETH	Arr.
FRED	I like you an' all.
BETH	Do ee, my dear? (*Sits on sofa.*)
FRED	Are, are you walking out with anyone?
BETH	No, I bain't.
FRED	Oh well—'ere—(*Sits beside her.*)
	(*They both grin.*)
	(*husky with emotion.*) Could I take you out like?
BETH	Arr.
FRED	When?
BETH	To-night.
FRED	Where?
BETH	(*moving into him quickly.*) Pictures!
FRED	(*almost on his back.*) What's on?
BETH	'It came from Outer Space.'
FRED	Did it? I mean, is it?
BETH	Arr. It's proper thrilling.
FRED	Oh, have you seen it?

BETH	Arr.
FRED	Who's in it?
BETH	I can't remember.
FRED	What's it about?
BETH	I can't remember.
FRED	Well, what was it thrilled you?
BETH	The man sitting beside me.
FRED	'Ere tha said tha wasn't walking out!
BETH	It's all right, my dear, I don't know who he was.
FRED	(*relieved.*) Oh. (*Realizes what she's said.*) Eh?
ALF	(*calls off.*) Fred!
FRED	Eh up. (*Jumps up.*)
BETH	Oh drat him. Don't forget to-night, will ee?
FRED	No, I won't. (*Moving to dining-room door.*)
BETH	Us'll have some rare fun. (*Winks.*) Pictures.
FRED	Aye, well, 'bye for now. (*Gives a little wave.*)
BETH	'Bye. (*Returns wave and blows a kiss.*)
FRED	'Bye.
	(FRED *returns kiss as* ALF *opens the door and taps* FRED *on the shoulder.* FRED *turns and in his blissful state blows a kiss to* ALF. ALF *hauls* FRED *off.*)
BETH	(*hugging her broom.*) You'm fatal to men, Beth my dear, fatal.
	(DANBY *comes downstairs with papers and account book. He overhears this last remark.*)
DANBY	I beg your pardon?
BETH	Oh, morning, Mr Danby.
DANBY	Good morning.
BETH	Shall I tell 'ee something?

DANBY	(*preoccupied with his work.*) Yes, do.
BETH	I've found a man!
DANBY	(*startled.*) Good God, where?
BETH	Right here.
DANBY	(*looking round.*) Here?
BETH	Arr.
DANBY	What have you done with him.
BETH	Nothing yet. I'm waiting till to-night.
DANBY	Then where are you going?
BETH	Pictures.
DANBY	Ye—what?
BETH	Pictures, that's where he's taking me.
DANBY	Oh, I see. (*Sits.*)
BETH	He's in love.
DANBY	Really, who with?
BETH	Me, of course.
DANBY	Oh yes, of course, stupid of me.
BETH	And I love 'im too.
DANBY	Oh, that's handy.
BETH	Was you ever in love?
DANBY	Well er—as a matter of fact, yes.
BETH	Fair churns your innards up, don't it?
DANBY	Er——it has rather a disturbing influence, certainly.
BETH	Oh dear, I think I'm going to 'ave another turn.
DANBY	Oh well, look while you're turning. I'll just get on with some work.
BETH	I've got me work to do too. Not in your way, dear, am I? (*She leans over him.*)
DANBY	No——not a bit.

BETH	Tell me if I am, won't 'ee?
DANBY	Yes, I will. You're in my way.
BETH	Well I'll go and get my duster and we can have a proper dust up! (*Exit.*)
	(*Enter* SUSAN.)
SUSAN	Hullo there!
DANBY	Oh, hullo.
SUSAN	Busy?
DANBY	Trying to be.
SUSAN	Oh. (*Moves to exit.*)
DANBY	Please don't go.
SUSAN	What?
DANBY	I mean don't go because of me. This is nothing very important, I'd just as soon find some excuse to forget about it.
SUSAN	(*good-naturedly.*) I've been called several things before, but never an excuse.
DANBY	I'm sorry. What I meant was I'd far rather talk to you. Please sit down.
SUSAN	Well, just for a minute. (*They sit on the couch.*)
DANBY	That's better. (*Re-enter* BETH *with duster.*)
SUSAN	I should be working, too, you know.
DANBY	You never seem to stop.
SUSAN	The novelty hasn't worn off, yet.
DANBY	It will.
SUSAN	How are you liking your job?
DANBY	Well, it would help if I knew what it was all about.
SUSAN	Don't you?
DANBY	Frankly, no. I know something about book-keeping but not book-making.

SUSAN	I think you're holding this post under false pretences.
DANBY	I quite agree. Mr Tubbe's had three days to find me out. But he doesn't seem in the least worried.
SUSAN	You know, I have my doubts about him.
DANBY	Oh.
SUSAN	He's very charming and amusing, but there's something phoney about him, especially his accent.
DANBY	I expect he suddenly made a packet at the game and wants to be accepted in wealthy circles.
SUSAN	He surely doesn't think we're a wealthy circle?
DANBY	Oh yes. He's always talking as though your father owns the Bank of England.
SUSAN	He does.
DANBY	Owns it?
SUSAN	Oh I thought you said owes the Bank of England.
	(BETH *buries her face in her feather duster and shakes with laughter.*)
DANBY	Beth! I should stop when you get to the core!
SUSAN	Just do the dusting.
BETH	Right. (*Returns to work.*)
DANBY	By the way, you don't happen to have any ghosts here as well as dry rot, do you?
SUSAN	Not that I know of.
DANBY	I seem to hear the most extraordinary sounds at night. As is someone was stumbling about.
SUSAN	I've never heard anything.
DANBY	Maybe you're a heavy sleeper. (*Moves closer to* SUSAN.)
SUSAN	Mm——like a log.

DANBY	A very charming one. (BETH *leans over the soft back between them and* DANBY's *elbow which is on the back of the sofa, slips off.*) What about Beth?
SUSAN	Have you heard it?
BETH	What?
SUSAN	This knocking.
BETH	No, but I'll go and see. (*Walks to front door.*)
SUSAN	No, I didn't mean——
BETH	(*opens door.*) There's nowt 'ere.
DANBY	No, I meant a general sort of knocking.
BETH	Where?
DANBY	Nowhere in particular.
SUSAN	All over.
DANBY	That's right.
SUSAN	At night.
	(BETH *looks blanker and blanker.*)
DANBY	A sort of stumbling.
SUSAN	He doesn't sleep well.
BETH	He doesn't sound well.
	(*She slams the front door in* COLONEL WAGSTAFF's *face as he is about to enter.* WAGSTAFF *knocks very loudly.*)
BETH	I 'eard summat then. (*She opens the door.*) 'Ullo, come in, sir.
WAGSTAFF	Next time I want my front teeth out, I'll let you know.
SUSAN	Hullo, Daddy, where have you been?
WAGSTAFF	Shopping. Ever since that grey bowler arrived we've been dashing around trying to find enough food to keep it air-borne. Whatever you give him he asks for more.
SUSAN	I wonder why he always has it in his room?

DANBY	Perhaps he has secret visitors from the underworld.
SUSAN	(*laughing.*) That would account for all those noises you hear.
WAGSTAFF	What noises?
SUSAN	Mr Danby says he can't sleep at night because of a rumbling.
BETH	Shouldn't eat cheese last thing. (*Exit with parcels U.L.*)
	(MR TUBBE *and* FRED *enter D.R.*)
ALF	Good morning to one and all.
ALL	Good morning, Mr Tubbe.
	(BETH *enters U.L.*)
ALF	What a beautiful day. How charming you look this morning, if I may say so.
WAGSTAFF	(*vaguely.*) Thanks very much.
SUSAN	Thank you. I hope you slept well.
ALF	Spark out, my dear. Spark out. (*Looks at his watch.*) Ah, time for tiffin, eh Colonel?
WAGSTAFF	That's not a bad idea.
ALF	Beth, two tiffins and soda.
FRED	I'll help you. (*Does so.*)
ALF	Many letters this morning, Danby?
DANBY	Yes, lots, mostly bets for the big race tomorrow. Everyone's on the French horse Cardinal.
ALF	Yes, the Cardinal's favourite. It's a fine horse. Magnificent horse.
DANBY	Will he win?
ALF	Not if I can hel——. (*Changing the subject.*) How did you sleep, my dear.
SUSAN	Very well, thanks.

ALF	That's right.
	(BETH *gives* ALF *a drink through the crook of his arm.*)
SUSAN	Poor Mr Danby didn't though.
ALF	Oh, and what's your trouble?
DANBY	A noise.
ALF	Oh. (*Takes a drink.*)
DANBY	As if someone was walking about.
	(ALF *splutters into his drink and* FRED *drops a bottle behind the bar.*)
ALF	Imagination. I never heard a thing.
FRED	Nor me.
ALF	Well, it's time we got to work. What a lovely morning for gardening, Colonel. I expect you want to be out digging. (*Takes his drink from him and goes to French windows.*)
WAGSTAFF	Yes, I think it——
ALF	Quite right. Get out there, and turn over. (*Almost pushes him into the garden.*)
	(*Exit* COLONEL WAGSTAFF.) Beth, you can do my room now, and do it thoroughly.
BETH	Right. (*Takes her broom and duster goes upstairs.*)
ALF	Danby, post these letters right away, please. They're urgent. (*Hands him a couple of letters.*)
DANBY	Right you are. Would you like a stroll, Miss Wagstaff?
SUSAN	No thanks. I've plenty of work to do in the kitchen.
DANBY	The kitchen'll still be there when you get back.
SUSAN	So will the work.
DANBY	Ah yes, but a ten minute walk down a leafy lane's a tonic.

SUSAN	With you?
DANBY	And the birds and the bees.
ALF	Aye, aye.
FRED	Aye.
SUSAN	No thank you, another time, perhaps.
DANBY	All right.
SUSAN	Give my love to all your feathered friends. (*She exits D.L.* DANBY *gazes after her.*)
ALF	Danby, are you still with us?
DANBY	Yes. (*Lost in a reverie.*)
ALF	Well you didn't oughter be!
	(DANBY *exits through front door.*)
FRED	That's got rid of that little lot, shall we knock him up now?
ALF	Yes, OK. (*Opens case and takes out a thermos, sandwiches and a plate of pudding.*) That should keep him going for another twelve hours. OK Operation Panel!
FRED	Righto, guv. (*Kicks, and panel opens.*)
ALF	(*calling softly.*) Flash, Flash. Grub's up. (*No sound.*)
FRED	'E must 'ave gone.
ALF	He can't have done.
FRED	P'raps he's asleep.
ALF	Flash. (*Whistles rather loudly.*)
	(BETH *appears on landing.*)
BETH	Were you calling?
FRED	(*whips round.*) No, no. Just a bird in the garden we've seen. (*Starts whistling.*)
BETH	That'll be little blackie, he comes along every morning. (*Also joins in whistling.*)

(FLASH's *head pops out.*)

ALF   (pushing FLASH *back.*) Get back! Er——get back
           to your work, Beth.

FRED   'Op it quick!

BETH   I like bird watching.

FRED   We'll watch this bird, thanks all the same.

BETH   If you want to feed it, I'll get some crusts.

FRED   It's all right, we've got coffee and sausages.

ALF   Eh!!

FRED   I mean——

           (FLASH *pops his head out again and* ALF *pushes it in.*)

ALF   Get back and finish my room, there's a good
           girl. We'll have another look at the birds later.
           It's flown off now anyway.

BETH   I know the one you mean, he's got a nest in the
           wall.

           (*Exits.* ALF *and* FRED *re-act.*)

FLASH   (*popping out again.*) Alf, I'm starving, where's the
           grub?

ALF   Sh! Here you are, for Gawd's sake 'urry. We
           can't play this game much longer. I think
           they're getting suspicious.

FLASH   (*drinks coffee from thermos.*) Why? They haven't
           seen me.

ALF   No, but they've heard you in the night.

FRED   Do you snore?

FLASH   Certainly not. (*Picking up a sandwich.*) What's
           these?

ALF   Bangers.

FLASH   Lovely. (*Bites it but doesn't seem to like it.*)

ALF   What's the matter?

FLASH   Where's the cosmetics?

ALF	For crying out loud, stuff it down! (*Forces sausage down* FLASH's *throat.*)
FLASH	That reminds me. I bumped my 'ead on something in there.
ALF	We'll have a doctor and two trained nurses standing by in future.
FLASH	No, listen, Alf, I think it's a lever, maybe it works the door from the inside.
FRED	(*nursing his foot.*) I'm all for that.
ALF	Let's have a look. (*They exit through panel.*)
FLASH	(*off, inside panel.*) 'Ere it is. I didn't dare try it before.
FRED	Pull it.
ALF	Won't budge.
FLASH	Well, push it.
ALF	Ah!
	(*The panel closes on all three.* MRS WAGSTAFF *enters from kitchen and sees the half-eaten food on the table.*)
MRS W	Well, really——. (*Calls.*) Beth! Beth!
	(BETH *appears.*)
BETH	Yes, my dear?
MRS W	What on earth is this doing here?
BETH	(*comes downstairs.*) I think it's for Mr Tubbe's birds.
MRS W	His what?
	(*The panel opens.* ALF *takes one look into the room and the panel closes.*)
BETH	For his birds.
MRS W	All of it? Well take it away. I'm having quite enough trouble trying to feed everyone, without bothering with our dumb friends in the garden. Where's the Colonel?

BETH	In the garden. (*Exits with food.*)
	(MRS WAGSTAFF *looks at her and then exits into the garden.* ALF, FRED *and* FLASH *emerge.*)
ALF	'Struth, that was close!
FRED	Well, you've had your breakfast! It's gone!
FLASH	I shall catch malnutrition.
ALF	Here, thinking of malnutrition, how's Sweet Lavender this morning?
FLASH	Alive.
ALF	Can he stand?
FLASH	Yes, if he leans on something.
ALF	What?
FLASH	No, he's all right.
ALF	Don't overdo the doping.
FLASH	No.
ALF	Remember he's got to be strong enough to run at Seldon.
FLASH	Well you can come and look after him for a bit then.
FRED	Oh no!
FLASH	Oh yes!
ALF	Come on, get back before they come in, and use that lever to open your front door with.
FLASH	But 'ow will I know if it's safe to come out.
ALF	I've got it, we'll tap on the panel three times and that means it's safe.
FRED	What if it isn't safe?
ALF	What? Oh well, we'll give one big knock.
FLASH	All right.
FRED	Let's try it and see if you can hear us.
FLASH	Right you are. (*Goes back into panel and shuts it.*)

ALF   'Ere goes. (*Knocks softly three times. No response.
            Knocks louder as ——)*

            (COLONEL *and* MRS WAGSTAFF *enter from the
            garden. They stand and gape.* FRED *turns and sees
            them.*)

FRED   Hullo, hullo. (*Gives one loud knock.*)

ALF   What are yer——

            (FRED *nudges him and he sees the intruders.*)

            Oh, yes. (*He also knocks once.*)

WAGSTAFF   What in the name of thunder's going on?

FRED   Just testing—er—for—er-dry rot.

WAGSTAFF   I beg your pardon?

ALF   Mr Phipps here is an authority on rot.

FRED   That's right, and knowing about the patch on
            the stairs. I was wondering if you had any more.

ALF   If it gets a hold it can be nasty, very nasty.

MRS W   I'm sure we haven't any more, have we, Henry?

WAGSTAFF   I don't think so. How can you tell?

FRED   Just by tapping. See. (*He knocks thrice.*) And then
            if——

            (*Panel opens slightly and* ALF *gives loud knock and it
            closes, unseen by the others.*)

            Then if you get a sort of hollow sound, you
            know what you've got.

WAGSTAFF   What?

ALF   Rot.

MRS W   Oh Henry, do let's make sure.

WAGSTAFF   Very well, dear.

            (*He also begins knocking. General pandemonium as
            COLONEL and MRS WAGSTAFF knock all over the
            walls, while ALF and FRED give the single knocks
            whenever the panel begins to open. BETH comes
            downstairs, thinks they've all gone mad, and edges her
            way into the kitchen.*)

I can't hear. Stop it, stop it! The whole thing is ridiculous.

(ALF *and* FRED *stand by panel on guard.*)

ALF   I should wait till we've gone and you're on your own.

WAGSTAFF   Heaven knows when that'll be. I feel we shall never have the place to ourselves again.

MRS W   Henry, what's to-day?

WAGSTAFF   Friday.

MRS W   That's what I thought. Seems odd.

WAGSTAFF   Not really, dear. Yesterday was Thursday.

MRS W   I seem to associate something with Friday, but I can't think what.

WAGSTAFF   Fish, probably.

(*Enter* DANBY *with some mail.*)

DANBY   Mr Tubbe anywhere?

ALF   What is it?

DANBY   Oh. I've just met the postman, there's another pile of letters for you.

ALF   All right, well open them.

(DANBY *sits.*)

Fred, give him a hand.

FRED   (*whispering.*) Yes, but what if——

ALF   We can't both stand here. Go on.

(FRED *sits by* DANBY *and helps.*)

MRS W   Well, I'm sure I don't know what it was.

WAGSTAFF   (*reading a paper*). What what was?

MRS W   Friday.

WAGSTAFF   Oh.

MRS W   I'll ask Beth. (*Exits.*)

(*Three loud knocks on the front door.* ALF *and* FRED *instinctively knock once. The letters fly out of* DANBY'S *hand.*)

WAGSTAFF   Don't start that again.

FRED   It's the front door.

             (*Another knock on the door.*)

WAGSTAFF   (*rising and going to door.*) It's like living in King's Cross.

FRED   Lovely spot. I lived there for six years.

             (WAGSTAFF *opens the front door. He is confronted with* ALBERT POLIGNAC, *a little Frenchman who speaks no English. So imagines, like the English, that as long as he shouts, he'll be understood. He is very quick and lively.*)

POLIGNAC   (*enters.*) Bonjour, Messieurs, que je suis heureux de me trouver ici à votre charmant hotel. Je m'appelle Polignac — Albert Polignac, mais sans doute vous me connaissez déjà —n'est-ce pas?

WAGSTAFF   I say, look here——

POLIGNAC   Alors, c'est qui le patron ici? Je dois absolument parler au patron. Ah c'est vous Monsieur. (*Rushes over to* ALF.) Enchanté de faire votre connaissance, je sens trés bien que je serai bien content ici chez vous. (*Shakes him warmly by the hand under the impression that he is the manager, being so much better dressed than* COLONEL WAGSTAFF, *who is in his shirt sleeves after gardening.*)

FRED   (*to* ALF.) Friend of yours?

ALF   Never seen the geezer.

FRED   'E seems to like you!

POLIGNAC   Comme je vous ai dit Monsieur, je ne serais ici que pour la nuit — je le regrette beaucoup.

FRED   Aye — that's right, aye.

WAGSTAFF   I say, who the devil is he, and what's he doing here?

POLIGNAC	(*angry.*) Ca n'est pas très poli ca! — qui est cet homme? Espérons que tous les domestiques ne soient pas pareils.
FRED	'Ere Danby, you ought to know what he's gabbling about.
DANBY	I only know a little French schoolboy. I mean a little schoolboy French.
FRED	French, is it, well that's something to go on. (*to* POLIGNAC.) Gay Paree and all that, yer know. Go on, guv., you have a bash.
ALF	That'll do, Phipps.
WAGSTAFF	I shan't ask many more times who the devil is it?
DANBY	I didn't catch the name, he spoke rather quickly.
WAGSTAFF	Well, tell him to start again.
DANBY	Yes — all right. (*With great reluctance.*) Er — encore s'il vous plait.
POLIGNAC	Pardon.
FRED	Granted.
ALF	Quiet.
DANBY	(*to* POLIGNAC.) Again, encore, encore.
FRED	(*clapping his hands.*) Bravo encore!
ALF	Phipps!
POLIGNAC	Je ne suis pas venu ici pour qu'on m'insulte c'est comme ca la politesse anglais.
WAGSTAFF	Look, tell him this is a hôtel.
DANBY	OK — er — c'est un hôtel ici, un hôtel.
POLIGNAC	Ah, ces anglais, mais naturellement c'est un hôtel je ne serais pas venu sans le sachant que c'est un hôtel. Un hôtel, oui! Un hôtel!
DANBY	Yes, well we all seem to be agreed on that point.
WAGSTAFF	For the last time, will you ask him who he is!

ALF	Whoo — are — yoooo!
DANBY	Name! Quel nom?
POLIGNAC	C'est à moi que vous le demande? A moi, le plus grand jockey de la France.
FRED	Well, we'll just call you 'Shorthouse.'
	(ALF *freezes* FRED *with a look.*)
DANBY	I don't think all that was his name.
WAGSTAFF	(*rushing over to* POLIGNAC.) Once and for all, who the devil are you?
POLIGNAC	Ne criez pas à moi, Monsieur!
WAGSTAFF	If you don't stop shouting I'll have you thrown out!
POLIGNAC	Mais jamais, jamais, on m'a traité ainsi.
WAGSTAFF	He's mad.
POLIGNAC	C'est formidable.
MRS W	(*entering with* SUSAN.) For goodness sake, Henry. What is all this shouting about?
POLIGNAC	(*not noticing ladies in his rage.*) Je m'en vais de refuse de rester encore un second. Je parlerai de vous. (*Sees the ladies and immediately advises them to leave the place.*) Chères mesdames, je vous conseil de fuir tout de suite, ici vous n'auriez que du mal. (*Tries to drag them away.*)
DANBY	Wait! Wait, this is the Manager's wife. Wife of manager — femme de Manager?
POLIGNAC	Femme du Manager?
DANBY	Oui, et she is the daughter, la fille.
POLIGNAC	Je suis enchanté de rencontrer deux dames si belles. (*Kissing their hands and hanging on to* SUSAN's *longer than necessary.*) Mademoiselle, vous me fait esprit encore.
DANBY	I say, let go!
POLIGNAC	(*returning to* MRS WAGSTAFF.) On soit très bien comme votre fille est si charmante. (*Kisses her hand again.*)

WAGSTAFF	Come away from my wife.
MRS W	Now Henry, be patient. I'm sure he's nearly finished. (*Smiles at* POLIGNAC.)
POLIGNAC	A votre service, madame. (*Kisses her again.*)
FRED	Would you like the salt and pepper?
WAGSTAFF	Will someone tell me, who is this idiot?
POLIGNAC	Idiot? Idiot?
ALF	That's torn it.
POLIGNAC	C'est cet idiot que se m'appeller idiot.
WAGSTAFF	If you don't ask him what his name is, I shall go stark, staring mad!
DANBY	Quel nom, monsieur?
ALF	(*joining in.*) Yer name —savez?
POLIGNAC	Mon dieu!
ALF	You'd have saved a lot of time if you'd said that before, Mr Mondure.
DANBY	No, I don't think that's quite right, sir. Pardon, Monsieur, votre nom?
POLIGNAC	Je vous le dirai pour la dernière fois. Polignac. Albert Polignac.
DANBY	Ah, good show, that's it, Albert Polignac.
WAGSTAFF	Well, you might ask Mr Polly — what he wants.
MRS W	Oh, Henry.
WAGSTAFF	What?
MRS W	Now I remember, it's that man — Friday!
WAGSTAFF	Man Friday?
SUSAN	The man that was coming on Friday.
WAGSTAFF	That was a jockey, not a Frenchman.
SUSAN	He could be both, ask him, Mr Danby.
DANBY	Est ce que——

POLIGNAC	Pardon?
ALF	(*to* POLIGNAC, *loudly.*) Jockey? You know, jo — keee — savez?
POLIGNAC	Comment?
ALF	I don't think he's French at all. (*Again loudly.*) Horses. You know, riding. (*He goes through the motions of riding.*)
WAGSTAFF	That's right, racing and all that. (*He also pretends to be riding and so do* FRED *and* DANBY.)
POLIGNAC	Ah oui (*he understands*) demain je gagnerai.
FRED	He's smiling; we're on to something now. (*Rushes over to* POLIGNAC *and kisses his hand.*) How d'you do? Phipps is my name. Monsure Phipps.
POLIGNAC	Pheeps?
FRED	No, Phipps.
POLIGNAC	Oui, Pheeps.
FRED	'Ere, not so much of the 'wee.' You're not so big yourself.
DANBY	Just a minute, perhaps he's riding the favourite in the big race to-morrow, it's a French horse.
ALF	No, it's being ridden by Poliggnack.
SUSAN	This is Poliggnack, only he prefers Polignac.
ALF	Good heavens, then he must be riding the Cardinal.
POLIGNAC	(*stung into action by the word.*) Cardinal, oui bien sûr, mon cheval c'est le Cardinal, la plus belle bête de la France et demain il ira comme une flèche d'or. (*With his hand he indicates great speed.*)
DANBY	I gather he's just gone past the winning post.
FRED	Oh no, he hasn't, 'cos we're going to switch the——
ALF	Switch the car on!!! (*Dives at* FRED, *who disappears out through the French windows.*)

Mrs W	Susan, go and tell Beth to show him to his room.
Susan	All right, mother. (*Exits.*)
Wagstaff	Well, he doesn't sound like a jockey to me.
Mrs W	Really, Henry, what do you expect him to do. Neigh?
Polignac	J'ai voyagé toute la nuit, je voudrais bien voir ma chambre. Je suis bien fatigué.
Wagstaff	What was all that about?
Danby	I think he said he was tired.
Wagstaff	I'm not surprised after all that talking.
Mrs W	Henry! (*To* Polignac.) I do apologize for my husband.
Polignac	Pardon?
Mrs W	My husband — er — mon——
Danby	Mari.
Mrs W	Mon mari.
Polignac	Votre mari?
Mrs W	Oui.
Polignac	Oh — le patron?
Mrs W	Oui.
Polignac	Oh monsieur, je suis desolé; je pensais que vous étiez le domestique. (*Kisses the Colonel on both cheeks.*)
	(*Enter* Beth.)
Mrs W	Beth, take this gentleman's case along to room Number Five.
Beth	Yes, me dear. (*To* Polignac.) This way.
Polignac	(*seeing her pick case up.*) Merci, Mademoiselle, merci.
Beth	Eh?

MRS W	He's French.
BETH	Oh, this way, Mr French (*She goes upstairs and* POLIGNAC *follows.*)
MRS W	Tell him to mind the dry rot, Mr Danby.
DANBY	Er — prenez garde — er——
POLIGNAC	Pardon. (*Stops.*)
DANBY	Don't rush me. Dry rot — er — dry — sec!
POLIGNAC	Sec?
DANBY	I haven't finished yet. Now 'rot.' Anyone know the French for rot?
WAGSTAFF	Composte?
DANBY	Composte. (*To* POLIGNAC.) Prenez garde sec composte.
POLIGNAC	Sec composte!
	(DANBY *points to* POLIGNAC's *foot. Lifts his foot and looks underneath it.*) Composte?
ALF	No, no. That's not it.
POLIGNAC	Les anglais! (*Takes one more step upstairs, and his foot goes clean through the woodwork and he lands with chin on the bannisters.*)
ALF	That's it!
POLIGNAC	(*waving his arms and swearing.*) Mon dieu, sacristi, nom de chien, zut, etc. . . .

THE CURTAIN FALLS

ACT TWO

Scene One

The early hours of the following morning. The stage is lit by moonlight.
FRED *is asleep on the couch. He's in his pyjamas and the jacket of his suit.*
ALF *comes to the head of the stairs with the attache case. Looks into the room.*
He is in shirt, trousers and dressing-gown and wearing his hat.

ALF	(*coming downstairs softly.*) Fred, Fred, are you there? (*Sees* FRED *and shakes him.*) Wake up!
FRED	(*shrieks.*) Ow!!

ALF	Sh! Want to wake the 'ole 'ouse? You're supposed to be guarding the panel.
FRED	I've been lying 'ere standing on guard for 'alf an 'our, me feet's gone quite blue. Look!
ALF	Quiet.
FRED	Got the grub?
ALF	Yes, and you can take over the watch while Flash has his supper. Poor old perisher, he's only 'ad 'alf a sausage for breakfast and that was fourteen hours ago. Now then. (*Knocks three times on the panel. Nothing happens. Knocks louder.*)
FRED	'E's never there when you want him.
ALF	No, and this morning he was popping in and out like a piston. Come on, Flash, for Gawd's sake. (*Knocks louder.*)
	(COLONEL WAGSTAFF *comes to the head of the stairs with a gun. He is in pyjamas.*)
WAGSTAFF	Who's there?
	(ALF *and* FRED *flatten themselves against the wall.*)
	I can hear you, don't move!
MRS W	(*off*) Henry, do come back to bed, you're imagining things.
	(*Panel opens and* FLASH *pops out.*)
ALF	(*in a whisper.*) Quiet!
	(ALF *and* FRED *grab his arms and hold him back.*)
MRS W	Henry!
WAGSTAFF	Sh! I tell you I heard something. I'm going to investigate.
MRS W	Do be careful.
WAGSTAFF	Don't worry, if I see anything I shall fire.
	(ALF, FRED *and* FLASH *dive into panel and almost shut it.* FRED *sneezes and panel shuts with a bang.*)
	Who's that? (*Comes downstairs slowly.*) Don't move! Where are you? (*He puts his foot through the hole in the stairs.*) Blast!!

(MRS WAGSTAFF *and* SUSAN *rush on.*)

MRS W	What's happened?
SUSAN	What have you done?
WAGSTAFF	Shut up! How can I possibly catch him with you shouting?
SUSAN	Catch who?
MRS W	Your father thinks he heard a burglar.
WAGSTAFF	I tell you, I distinctly.——
MRS W	Yes, all right, dear. It's all over now. Do take your foot out of there and come back to bed.

(SUSAN *puts the lights on.*)

WAGSTAFF	I'm going to find him.
MRS W	You won't be able to see a thing now. Have a look in the morning when it's light.
WAGSTAFF	He'll be gone by then!
MRS W	A good thing too. Now, come on.
WAGSTAFF	I'm stuck. (*Struggling to try and free himself.*)

(DANBY *arrives on the scene.*)

DANBY	I say, what's going on? A fire or something?
SUSAN	No. Daddy thought he heard a burglar.
WAGSTAFF	I did hear one.
DANBY	That's bad, anything missing?
SUSAN	Only his foot so far — it's wedged in the dry rot.
DANBY	Good Lord, are you stuck, sir?
WAGSTAFF	No, dear boy. I always sleep in this position. Don't just stand there, do something.
DANBY	Hold on, I'll pull. (*Does so.*)
WAGSTAFF	Ow!! Steady on!
MRS W	Henry, you'll catch your death of cold if you stand there much longer.

WAGSTAFF	Dammit, woman, I can't move!
SUSAN	Look, Mummy, you take one arm, I'll take the other, and Mr. Danby, you hold him round the middle. Right now, pull.
WAGSTAFF	Owww!!
MRS W	That's no good.
DANBY	It's wedged all right. Have you got a saw?
WAGSTAFF	Sore what?
DANBY	No, I mean a saw — you know — for sawing.
WAGSTAFF	What are you going to do — amputate?
DANBY	I thought we might widen the hole.
MRS W	What are we going to do?
SUSAN	I'll go and make some tea, shall I?
WAGSTAFF	You may as well get the cards out, too.
	(SUSAN *exits.*)
DANBY	I've got hold of something. (*With his hand in the hole.*)
WAGSTAFF	Ow! Yes, you have.
DANBY	There's a bar across your foot. Now if I can lift it up a bit, you can pull your foot up. Ow! Not yet. My hand's jammed now.
WAGSTAFF	Oh Lord!
DANBY	Push your leg down. That's better. Now, I'll lift the bar and you take his arm, Mrs Wagstaff. You all right, sir?
WAGSTAFF	Yes, enjoying every minute of it.
DANBY	Ready. Heave!
	(WAGSTAFF *comes shooting out.*)
WAGSTAFF	Thank you.
	(DANBY's *arm is now jammed in the hole.*)
MRS W	Thank heavens! Now come along, Henry, and another time don't rush into these things.

WAGSTAFF	Into what things?
DANBY	(*in difficulty*). Er — I say——
MRS W	Next time you think you hear someone——
WAGSTAFF	Doris, if you say I imagine it once more——
DANBY	(*tapping* COLONEL WAGSTAFF's *leg.*) Excuse me, sir——
WAGSTAFF	What?
DANBY	Could you give me a hand?
WAGSTAFF	Why?
DANBY	I seem to have lost one!
MRS W	Oh do get up, there's a good boy.
DANBY	I'd love to, only I'm stuck.
MRS W	Oh not again. Henry, help Mr. Danby up.
	(*They both pull and* DANBY *is released.*)
DANBY	Ah, thanks. (*counts his fingers.*) One, two, three, four, five, yes we're all here.
MRS W	Good. Now let's go back to bed before we all catch pneumonia.
WAGSTAFF	I shall get on to the police about this.
MRS W	Yes dear, in the morning! Don't disturb them now.
DANBY	Good-night.
MRS W	Good night. Come along, Henry.
	(COLONEL *and* MRS WAGSTAFF *exit.* DANBY *is about to follow when* SUSAN *comes back from the kitchen.*)
SUSAN	Kettle won't be a moment. I — oh.
DANBY	Hullo. Emergency's over.
SUSAN	Oh, then I'd better go and turn it out.
DANBY	Must you?
SUSAN	It'll boil dry.

DANBY	I mean, must you go at this moment?
SUSAN	(*a little bewildered.*) Huh?
DANBY	You look so lovely. D'you know something?
SUSAN	What?
DANBY	I'm glad your father heard a burglar.
SUSAN	Why?
DANBY	If he hadn't we shouldn't be standing here now.
SUSAN	I'm not sure we ought to be, burglar or no burglar. It's not a habit of mine to talk with strange men in dressing-gowns at two a.m.
DANBY	I'll take it off if you like. (*Then suddenly realizes what he's said.*) But I wouldn't say I was a stranger. We've known each other for three whole days.
SUSAN	Practically a lifetime!
DANBY	You can know someone as well in three days as you can in three months. It all depends how hard you concentrate.
SUSAN	(*with a chuckle.*) How long do you feel you've known me?
DANBY	Six months at least.
SUSAN	Your powers of concentration must be enormous.
DANBY	They are.
SUSAN	And don't you think after all that concentration you ought to go to bed and give your mind a rest?
DANBY	Oh I do some of my most valuable work when I'm asleep; there's nothing to distract me so I can devote all my dreams to you.
SUSAN	(*slightly embarrassed.*) I think perhaps I'd better see to that kettle.
DANBY	I'll help you. Don't forget we've had burglars.

SUSAN	Not in the kitchen.
DANBY	I hope you're right! Come on.
	(*Exeunt. The panel opens and* FRED *peers out.*)
FRED	All clear.
ALF	Right. Come on, Flash, and for Gawd's sake, get this meal down quick. (*Opens the case.*)
FLASH	Ta.
ALF	Go on, Fred, you take over down there for a bit.
FRED	I'm losing all me sleep.
ALF	If you don't hurry up you'll lose all your beauty as well. Go on.
FRED	If you're going to be nasty I won't do it!
ALF	Sh!
FRED	Say Please.
ALF	Please.
FRED	Say it nicely.
ALF	(*spits it out.*) Please!
FLASH	'Ere, you're soakin' me sandwich.
ALF	For Pete's sake clear off. (*Bundles* FRED *into the panel.*) How's Sweet Lavender?
FLASH	I'm worried.
ALF	'Asn't rallied again, 'as he?
FLASH	No.
ALF	What then?
FLASH	I think we're overdoing the drugs.
ALF	He's still breathing — ain't he?
FLASH	(*doubtfully*). Well——
ALF	What d'yer mean, well?
FLASH	He goes for hours sometimes without moving a muscle.

| ALF | Better give him something to pep him up. The Cardinal's arriving to-morrer and Sweet Lavender will 'ave to be fit enough to be switched and taken on to the course as the Cardinal. |

FLASH   Well, he certainly don't look much like a 'wonder' horse at the moment.

ALF   Well, he's got to or his jockey'll get suspicious.

FLASH   Oh, I'd forgotten about the jockey. I don't think he could cope with one of them.

ALF   Eh?

FLASH   I showed him the saddle just now and he rolled up his eyes and said 'neigh.'

ALF   Said 'nay'?

FLASH   Yes. (*Demonstrates.*) Ne-e-e-igh!

ALF   Shut up!

(*Noises off.* SUSAN *and* DANBY *returning.*)

Blimey, look out, duck — hide!

(*General scamble as they conceal themselves behind the furniture* ALF *behind couch and* FLASH *behind bar.*)

(DANBY *enters with* SUSAN.)

DANBY   I think that was the nicest cup of tea I ever had.

SUSAN   Me, too, now don't you think we'd better say good-night?

DANBY   Frankly, no.

SUSAN   (*firmly.*) Good night.

DANBY   'Good?' It's beautiful.

SUSAN   Come on.

DANBY   No hurry. What time's breakfast?

SUSAN   About nine, why?

DANBY   Then we've got six clear hours in which to say good night.

ALF   (*behind a chair.*) Oh Gawd!

SUSAN   I think that might get a trifle monotonous. Good
               night, Mr. Danby.

DANBY   G'night, Miss Wagstaff. (DANBY *sees the top of
               ALF's bowler hat sticking up above the arm of the couch
               and thinks it must be on little table.*) Oh, Mr.
               Tubbe's left his hat down here. (*Leans over, lifts it
               clean off his head, hangs it up and goes upstairs.*) Miss
               Wagstaff?

SUSAN   Yes?

DANBY   Can I call you Susan?

SUSAN   Yes — please.

DANBY   G'night, Susan.

SUSAN   G'night, John. (*She walks off, the men emerge.*)

DANBY   Susan?

               (*Men shoot back again.*)

SUSAN   Yes, John?

DANBY   How about 'Sue?'

SUSAN   All right, 'Jo.'

DANBY   'Night, Sue.

SUSAN   'Night, Jo.

               (*Exeunt.*)

FLASH   Alfred?

ALF   Careful, he might call her back and give her a
               number.

FLASH   Alfred, can I call you Alf? (*Panel opens.* FRED
               enters.)

FRED   (*agitated.*) Guv.

ALF   What's up?

FRED   Sweet Lavender——

ALF   What?

FRED	He's unconscious.
FLASH ALF }	Unconscious?
FRED	Aye, he's right bad.
ALF	You clumsy idiot. That's ten thousand pounds you've just thrown away.
FRED	(*genuinely moved.*) Poor thing——
ALF	It's us that's poor!
FLASH	I thought he looked a bit dicky when he went ne-e-e-igh!
ALF	Oh shut up! Ten thousand nicker down the drain and you stand there making bloody silly noises! That ruddy wonder horse'll win now. We've got nothing to switch it with.
FLASH	We'll 'ave to nobble it.
ALF	On no — that's illegal.
FLASH	'Ere wait, we needn't bother with the 'orse at all. We've got the jockey 'aven't we?
ALF	So what?
FRED	All we 'ave to do is keep Polignack 'ere till the race is over and Bob's your uncle!
ALF	That's no good, if the Cardinal don't run then I lose all the money that I bet on him and we don't get no ten thousand pounds! Cardinal's gotter run, but he's gotter lose.
FRED	Gotter run, but he's gotter lose. (*Thinking.*)
FLASH	I've got it. We nab the Frenchman, Polignack, then put in a substitute jockey.
ALF	Yus. That's it.
FRED	Aye, but who?
ALF	Doesn't matter who, so long as he can't ride very well and isn't known on the course.
FLASH	That lets me out, if I go near the place I'd be clapped in irons.

ALF	And me. I'm a bit heavy, too.
FRED	Aye. Now who do we know that's not known, not 'eavy and can't ride?

(ALF *and* FLASH *both look at* FRED.)

FLASH	Can't ride well!!
ALF	Not 'eavy!
FRED	Oh no! No, no, not me. I'm not goin' on any 'orse, for anyone.
ALF	Quiet! Quiet! Look out, someone's coming.

(*There is a bang upstairs.* ALF *and* FRED *duck in front of couch.* FLASH *dives into panel.* POLIGNAC *comes downstairs. It is obvious what he's looking for. Just as he gets to the panel* FLASH *emerges. He swerves past* FLASH, *goes to door U.L., opens it, peers in, closes it. He comes back to* FLASH *who taps him on the shoulder and points to door D.L.* POLIGNAC *looks relieved and dashes off D.L. and exits.*)

(ALF *and* FRED *Stay in their positions and continue their discussion and* FLASH *joins them.*)

FLASH	Fred, you've gotter do it!
FRED	Look 'ere, guv., you can find yourself another mug.
ALF	Fred, it's money for jam.
FLASH	You'd be doing us all a favour.
FRED	Aye and myself a permanent injury.
ALF	I'll give you half the profits. You'll be rich.
FLASH	Able to afford anything.
ALF	A lovely wedding.
FRED	An expensive funeral!
ALF	Don't talk so wet, Fred.
FRED	No!
FLASH	Fred——

FRED	No!
ALF	Fred——
FRED	You can 'Fred' me till you're blue in the face but——
WAGSTAFF	(*off-stage.*) Who's that! Doris, where's my gun? He's back. I'll get him this time.
	(ALF, FLASH and FRED *exit through French windows, panel and dining-room as* COLONEL WAGSTAFF *enters.*)
	Who's there? There's a gang of them — Doris!
MRS W	(*off.*) Not again, Henry!
WAGSTAFF	Keep back, dear, we're being besieged. Get under cover. I'll phone the police. (*Lifts the receiver.*)
BETH	(*rushing on* D L *in a nightdress.*) I can't sleep, what's going on?
WAGSTAFF	We're being raided. Take my gun and cover the doors with it. (*Into phone.*) Get me police!
	(BETH *rushes madly round with the gun, pointing it with bared teeth at all the doors.*)
	Ah Police, come at once to the 'Bull and Cow,' we're being attacked from all points. (*Bangs down receiver. Whips round and impales himself on the gun.*) Idiot!
BETH	Sorry.
WAGSTAFF	Give it here, get a broom or a poker. (BETH *exists* D L).
	(DANBY *and* SUSAN *enter.*)
DANBY	What's happened?
WAGSTAFF	Ah, Danby, barricade the doors and grab something heavy. Susan, get with your mother.
SUSAN	What is it?
WAGSTAFF	I was right after all.
SUSAN	About a burglar?

(*Enter* MRS WAGSTAFF.)

WAGSTAFF   A burglar? There are hordes of 'em. They were
            charging all over the room. Has everyone got a
            weapon, Beth? (BETH *enters.*)

BETH   Aye, 'ere you are, Miss. (*Hands her a feather duster
            from behind the bar.*)

SUSAN   What am I supposed to do with this?

WAGSTAFF   Grab something heavy. Doris, have you got
            anything?

MRS W   No, dear.

WAGSTAFF   Well, get something!

MRS W   I'll get the tea, shall I. (*Goes* D L)

WAGSTAFF   Tea? Your lives are in danger and you talk
            about tea.

DANBY   How about a whisky, sir?

WAGSTAFF   Ah, good idea, steady the nerves. Beth, whisky!

            (MRS WAGSTAFF *exsts* D L)

WAGSTAFF   Never mind the barricades, Danby, just make
            sure you're armed, and take up your positions.
            Sue, dining-room, Danby, front door, and I'll
            take the French windows.

MRS W   (*off.*) Henry!! (SUSAN *and* DANBY RUSH *off* D L.)

WAGSTAFF   Coming, Doris, coming. (*Rushing off.*)

BETH   Your whisky, sir.

WAGSTAFF   No time, come on. (*Exits.*)

            (BETH *puts it on the table and rushes off after the
            others.* ALF *comes through windows looking miserable.
            Sees whisky and drinks it.*)

DANBY   (*off.*) I'll nip back, sir. Come on, Sue.

WAGSTAFF   Be careful. (*Off.*)

            (ALF *exits as* SUSAN *enters followed by* DANBY.)

SUSAN   There he goes!!

DANBY	I'll see, don't go out. (*Rushes out through French windows.*)
	(COLONEL WAGSTAFF, MRS WAGSTAFF *and* BETH *re-enter.*)
MRS W	(*entering.*) I tell you I saw a man. I was terrified.
WAGSTAFF	Whisky, quick.
	(BETH *picks up the glass from the table thinking it is full.*)
SUSAN	What did he look like?
MRS W	It was too dark to see.
WAGSTAFF	(*taking glass from* BETH.) Here, drink this.
MRS W	Drink what? (*Looking at the glass.*)
WAGSTAFF	Beth, fill it up, you fool! (*Enter* DANBY.) See anyone?
DANBY	No, he's done a floon-light mit—er—moon—light flit!
SUSAN	Come along, mother, I'll take you back to bed.
WAGSTAFF	It's not safe to move from here, if we stay together we may have a chance.
	(*Three loud knocks on the front door.*)
	Take cover!
	(*Everyone dives on to the floor. Three more knocks, panel opens,* FLASH *comes out, sees everyone on the floor so goes in again and panel shuts. All unseen. More knocking.*)
DANBY	Maybe it's the police, sir.
WAGSTAFF	I'll see, you stay put. Beth, take my gun and keep me covered.
	(*He opens the door and is confronted with an enormous policewoman,* SERGEANT FIRE *by name, with a voice of thunder.*)
FIRE	About time!
WAGSTAFF	Uh?

FIRE	Understand you rang for help?
WAGSTAFF	I rang the police.
FIRE	I am the police, Sergeant Fire reporting.
WAGSTAFF	It's absurd.
FIRE	Shush! What's the matter with all these people? (*Everyone is still on the floor.*) Are they dead?
WAGSTAFF	Certainly not.
FIRE	Get up. Now make your statement.
WAGSTAFF	The house is surrounded by crooks, but why the devil they've sent you I can't imagine.
FIRE	Shush! (*Spraying all and sundry.*)
WAGSTAFF	Don't shush at me. I was a Colonel in the Army.
FIRE	I was a Brigadier in the A.T.S. Sit down!
WAGSTAFF	Now look here, Miss — Miss——
FIRE	Fire!
WAGSTAFF	Fire!
	(BETH *fires the gun off straight through the French windows. The Colonel and the Sergeant throw their arms round each other, and the others dive on to the floor.*)
WAGSTAFF	Idiot! (*Takes gun from* BETH.)
FIRE	Give me that. (*Takes gun from* COLONEL.)
	(ALF *comes hustling through the windows, holding his hat out, which has a hole in it.*)
ALF	Here, I've had enough, clean through my hat it went.
FIRE	You're under arrest.
ALF	Eh, what for?
DANBY	He lives here.
FIRE	Shush! Where's the rest of your gang?

ALF	(*calling out in direction of dining-room.*) Fred, better come in before they blow your 'ead off.
	(FRED *enters.*)
WAGSTAFF	Sergeant, I think there's been a mistake.
ALF	You think there has! What about me? (*Holding out his hat.*)
FIRE	Shush! You others go to bed. Off you go. (*She rounds them up with her gun.*)
	(ALL: *General protest as they go upstairs.*)
	Go to bed. (*Hits floor with rifle butt three times.*)
	(*Panel opens.* ALF *and* FRED *dash over and drape the dressing-gown which* ALF *still has on, over the panel.*)
	Come here, what are you doing?
ALF	Getting ready to go to bed.
FIRE	(*to* FRED.) And you?
FRED	I'm assisting him. I'm his Welsh dresser.
FIRE	Come here. (*Grabs the gown away, but panel is now shut.*)
WAGSTAFF	What the devil are you two doing up at this hour?
FIRE	I'll deal with them. Get to your rooms, all of you.
	(*Everyone goes upstairs and exits except the Colonel.*)
	(ALF *and* FRED *try to sneak off too.*)
	Not you. (*She grabs them.*)
WAGSTAFF	(*still not going.*) I want a full explanation. Mr Tubbe, this house has——
FIRE	Shush! What were you doing in the garden?
ALF	Sowing.
WAGSTAFF	At three in the morning?
ALF	They're early seeds.

FIRE	(*to* FRED.) And you?
FRED	Weeding.
WAGSTAFF	Why weren't you in bed?
FRED	Well, I don't weed in bed!
WAGSTAFF	You're lying.
FRED ALF }	Shush!
WAGSTAFF	How dare you shout at me. I——
FIRE	Sir, you're interfering with the law.
WAGSTAFF	Wha——
FIRE	If you persist I shall arrest you!
WAGSTAFF	It's an outrage. I shall report you!
FIRE	I've never been spoken to like this before!
WAGSTAFF	Well, make the most of it. I haven't finished.
	(*During this tirade* ALF *and* FRED *quietly exit* U.L. FIRE *and* WAGSTAFF *bear down on each other in turn.*)
FIRE	Don't you wag your finger at me. I've got a gun, remember.
WAGSTAFF	I don't care if you've got an arsenal; anyway, it's my gun, give it to me!
FIRE	I'll do no such thing.
WAGSTAFF	Give it me.
FIRE	No I won't, you're a maniac, that's what you are — a maniac.
WAGSTAFF	A what!! (*Grabs her arms.*)
FIRE	Probably a sex maniac!!!
WAGSTAFF	How dare you!!!!
	(*They part.* POLIGNAC *creeps out of the kitchen and stands watching the scene in complete amazement.*)
FIRE	Women are not safe with lunatics like you around.

WAGSTAFF	Lunatics!
FIRE	Get back or I'll shoot.
WAGSTAFF	Put it down.
	(*They come to grips and sway around.*)
FIRE	Get away, you dirty old man.
	(MRS WAGSTAFF *appears on the stairs and is horrified.*)
MRS W	HENRY!!

(WAGSTAFF *looks up and then they all see* POLIGNAC. MRS WAGSTAFF *points and shouts, 'That's him!' Whereupon* POLIGNAC, *terrified, turns and runs before he is recognised. He charges upstairs and off — followed by* WAGSTAFF *and* FIRE. SERGEANT FIRE *puts her foot firmly down the hole in the stairs and shoots for help as* ——)

THE CURTAIN FALLS

Scene Two

The same, the following morning. There is a red flag tied to the banisters to mark the hole.

SUSAN *is writing.* BETH *is sweeping up.* MRS WAGSTAFF *enters from the kitchen with a breakfast tray.*

MRS W	Beth, take this up to that Fire woman, she won't be able to budge an inch with that ankle.
BETH	That woman policeman?
MRS W	Yes.
BETH	I don't fancy goin' in there, she's a bit wild.
MRS W	Very well, I'll go, and you can take this up to Colonel Wagstaff instead.
BETH	(*dreading that even more.*) It's all right, give it 'ere. I'd rather face the firewoman! (*Exits upstairs.*)
SUSAN	I don't feel we shall ever get back to normal.
MRS W	Nor I.
SUSAN	A crippled policewoman in one room, an

	outraged Colonel in another and a selection of the most suspicious-looking characters I've ever seen spread over the rest of the house.
Mrs W	I'm worried. Do you think there's something going on? Something we don't know about?
Susan	I should just worry over the things we do know about.
Mrs W	I think I'll phone the police and get them to remove that woman. Oh, but wait a bit, there's your father's breakfast.
Susan	I'll see to it. You sit down for a bit. Where are the others?
Mrs W	Mr Tubbe and his little friend are in there — (*points to dining-room*) and the jockey and Mr Danby haven't come down yet.
Susan	Do you like John?
Mrs W	John? Who's John?
Susan	Mr Danby
Mrs W	He doesn't seem as crazy as the others.
Susan	(*gazing into space.*) I think he's rather charming.
Mrs W	Yes, I sup——. (*Looks at* Susan) For heaven's sake, girl, what are you talking about?
Susan	John.
Mrs W	You've only known him three days.
Susan	You can get to know someone as well in three days as you can in three months.
Mrs W	What?
Susan	It all depends how hard you concentrate.
Mrs W	Really.
Susan	And you can do some of your most valuable work in bed.
Mrs W	Susan! What in heaven's name are you talking about?
Susan	Dreams. (*Suddenly coming out of her trance and*

realizing what she's said.) Er—dreams, Mother, I was just day dreaming.

MRS W   Are you feeling quite well?

SUSAN   Yes, of course I am.

MRS W   Well, you don't sound it.

SUSAN   I'll go and get Daddy's tray. (*Exits.*)

MRS W   I do hope she's not sickening for anything. Now what—Oh yes, the police. (*She goes to the telephone and lifts receiver.*) Hullo. Get me the police, please. Hullo, is that the fire station—I mean the police station! Oh good—well now we've got that Fire woman of yours and we'd be glad if you'd collect her as soon as possible.

(SERGEANT FIRE *comes to the landing, hears the conversation and listens.*)

Look, have you or have you not a woman policman by the name of Fire working for you? Yes, well she's here and we'd rather she wasn't. At the 'Bull and Cow'—I'm not interested in why she came, and all she succeeded in doing was to put her foot through the stairs—at three o'clock—of course she's out now. Just come and claim her, that's all I'm asking. Thank you. (*Hangs up.*) Really, it's like talking to children. (*Exits.*)

(FIRE *now limps downstairs and makes for the phone.*)

FIRE   (*lifts receiver, and then in a loud whisper.*)

Hullo. Police station, quick. Hullo—Sergeant Fire reporting. Pay no attention to the previous call, leave me just where I am, I think I'm on to something pretty big. (*Placing her hand on her behind.*) The place is full of suspicious characters—it's run by a sex maniac, well, he attacked me—yes, me!!—possibly a white-slaver. No, I can't see any girls, but all the men seem to be raving lunatics. Right, I'll lie low, don't come near till you hear from me again. (*Replaces receiver and walks back upstairs, and meets DANBY who is coming down.*)

DANBY	Good morning, how's the ankle?
FIRE	Awful.
DANBY	Let me help you.
FIRE	Keep your hands off me!
DANBY	But I only want to——
FIRE	I know what you want, but you've met your match. I'm not to be trifled with. (*Exits*.)

(DANBY *comes down and glances at the mail.* SUSAN *enters with tray*.)

SUSAN	Oh, good morning.
DANBY	Hullo, Sue, how are you?
SUSAN	Fine, and you?
DANBY	I feel I've lost a little sleep somewhere.
SUSAN	Me too.
DANBY	You look as fresh as a rose and twice as lovely.
SUSAN	I must take this up.
DANBY	I'll do it. (*Takes tray*.)

(COLONEL WAGSTAFF *appears on the landing, is about to shout but sees the lovers below gazing at each other, and he looks from one to the other during the following dialogue*.)

SUSAN	No, it's all right. (*Takes tray*.)
DANBY	Sue?
SUSAN	Yes, John?
DANBY	I dreamt about you last night.
SUSAN	Did you?
DANBY	Yes (*takes tray*), but it wasn't very satisfactory. I'd just asked you a question and before you could answer I woke up. Stupid of me, wasn't it?
SUSAN	Depends, you might have got the wrong answer.
DANBY	I think I'll find out now. Are you listening?
SUSAN	Yes, John.

(*They are both holding the tray now.*)

DANBY   Right, we're back in the dream, and I say to you: 'Susan,' and you say——

SUSAN   Yes, John?

DANBY   And I say may I kiss you and you say——

SUSAN   Yes, John.

(*They kiss across the tray.*)

WAGSTAFF   Game and set!

(DANBY *and* SUSAN *jump.*)

Now, look here, Danby, I can't throw you out, much as I'd like to, because you're not entirely to blame for this nauseating little scene.

DANBY   But, Mr——

WAGSTAFF   But if there's any more nonsense I shan't hesitate to show you the door.

DANBY   But I——

WAGSTAFF   You've said quite enough. Now if you can both bear to part with that tray I'd like some breakfast.

SUSAN   I'll bring it up. (*She does so.*)

WAGSTAFF   Thank you.

(*They exit.* DANBY *sits down, looking miserable.* ALF *enters from dining-room, with attache case and hat.*)

ALF   Morning, Danby.

DANBY   (*gloomily.*) Morning.

ALF   Any mail?

DANBY   Yes.

ALF   Splendid, is there much? (*No reply.*) Ere, laughin' boy, I'm speaking to you.

DANBY   Oh. I—er—don't know yet.

ALF   The great day's here at last. (*Still* DANBY *just sits and stares.*) Not keeping you up, am I?

DANBY   I'm sorry, you were saying——

ALF   Yes, I was, but doesn't matter. Look, hop in the
             car and buy me a French phrase book. I'm
             thinking of taking a little holiday there soon.
             Just want to brush up the lingo. Hurry!

DANBY   All right. (*Exits.*)

             (*Enter* FLASH *from upstairs, carrying mackintosh and
             case.*)

FLASH   (*leans over bannister.*) Psst! (ALF *thinks it's raining
             and puts out his hand.*) 'Ere look, I've got
             Polignac's knick-knacks 'ere, it's got all racing
             stuff in it.

ALF   'Ow d'you manage that?

FLASH   Well, I knew we'd have to get 'old of them
             sometime before he left, so I just offered to carry
             'em down for him.

ALF   Good boy. (*Opening it and pulling out the jockey's
             outfit.*) Fred better try these on for size. Give 'im
             a call.

FLASH   O.K. Fred! (*At the foot of the stairs.*)

ALF   (*holding up silk blouse.*) He'll look a treat in these,
             won't he?

FLASH   Oh yes. Very French.

             (*Enter* FRED.)

FRED   What?

ALF   Come and try on your party dress.

FRED   'Ere, I'm not wearing that.

FLASH   Come on, it's your racing colours. (*Pulling his
             coat off.*)

FRED   I'm not going in any race.

ALF   Now look 'ere, Fred, you're in this up to your
             neck whether you like it or not. And if I say
             you're going to do it, you're going to do it.

FRED   I'll go to't police.

ALF	Oh, will you! Then I'll have to tell 'em all about a doped race'orse you 'ad tucked away.
FRED	I never doped it.
FLASH	You was with it.
ALF	Nasty charge, doping horses.
FRED	But I——
FLASH	You're an 'assassery' after the fact.
FRED	But——
ALF	Shut up and get changed. (FRED *is now in vest and trousers.*) We're paying you well, ain't we?
FRED	Ee—you're tickling me.
ALF	Well, do it yourself. (*His trousers are now down.*)
	(*Enter* FIRE *on the stairs. She gasps and exits.*)
MRS W	(*off.*) Mr Tubbe?
ALF	Look out!
FLASH	Quick! (*Throws mackintosh over* FRED. ALF *puts his hat on* FRED *and thrusts an attache case into his hand.*)
FRED	'Ere, what's going on? (*The hat is well down over his eyes.*)
	(FLASH *has shoved all the clothes into the case.*)
MRS W	Who's this?
ALF	Er—the piano tuner.
MRS W	Piano tuner?
ALF	That's right. (*To* FRED) You are, aren't you?
FRED	No.
	(ALF *digs him in the ribs.*)
ALF	Yes.
FRED	Yes.
MRS W	Well, what are you doing here?
ALF	He was sent for.

MRS W	Sent for?
FRED	Sent for.
MRS W	From here?
ALF	From here.
MRS W	Who by?
FLASH	Who were you sent here from for to by?
FRED	Eh?
FLASH	I'm not saying that again.
ALF	Colonel Wagstaff sent for him, didn't he?
FRED	Yes, Colonel Wagstaff.
MRS W	But this is ridiculous.
ALF	Yes, isn't it?
MRS W	I'm afraid the strain must have been too much for him. We haven't got a piano.
FRED	That's a bit of luck.
MRS W	What?
ALF	He means it's lucky he found out in time. He'd have pulled the place apart. He's so keen, aren't you?
FRED	Yes.
MRS W	Well, I'm sorry, but you'd better go back.
ALF	Yes, I think he had.
MRS W	I'm sorry you've been sent out here for nothing.
FRED	That's all right.
WAGSTAFF	(off-stage.) Doris!
ALF	(quickly.) Well, I shouldn't waste any more time, we'll see you on to a bus.
MRS W	There are no buses.
ALF	That's all right, he came on a tricycle.
	(FLASH and ALF hustle him out through the front door.)

WAGSTAFF	(*entering.*) Doris, where the devil's my scarf got to?
MRS W	Never mind about your scarf, come here, dear.
WAGSTAFF	(*comes down.*) What is it?
MRS W	How long have we been in this house?
WAGSTAFF	Six months. Why?
MRS W	Do you remember seeing a piano?
WAGSTAFF	Piano!
MRS W	Yes, dear, because I wish you'd show me where it is.
WAGSTAFF	You feeling all right?
MRS W	Perfectly.
WAGSTAFF	These last few days haven't overstrained you?
MRS W	No, Henry.
WAGSTAFF	Oh.
MRS W	Now, about this piano.
WAGSTAFF	(*convinced that her mind is wandering, humours her.*) Yes, dear?
MRS W	Where is it?
WAGSTAFF	Where is it?
MRS W	Take a good look round. Can you see it?
WAGSTAFF	Not at the moment.
MRS W	It doesn't exactly hit you in the eye, does it?
WAGSTAFF	Not exactly. Perhaps it's in the dining room.
MRS W	There's no room for it there.
WAGSTAFF	We might shift the furniture about.
MRS W	Henry, the point I'm trying to make is that we have no piano.
WAGSTAFF	Would you like one?
MRS W	No thank you.

WAGSTAFF	Oh.
MRS W	So how can we have it tuned?
WAGSTAFF	It is a bit of a problem.
MRS W	It would be, for the piano tuner.
WAGSTAFF	Quite.
MRS W	So there's not much point in his coming, is there?
WAGSTAFF	No, not really.
MRS W	Well, that's a relief.
WAGSTAFF	*(still very worried about his wife.)* Now Doris, stop worrying about the piano and come and lie down.
MRS W	Oh, it's all over now.
WAGSTAFF	I'm very relieved to hear it.
MRS W	But it's a long way to come for nothing on a tricycle!
WAGSTAFF	Eh!!
	(MRS WAGSTAFF *exits upstairs.* POLIGNAC *comes downstairs with a grip.*)
POLIGNAC	Bonjour, monsieur, bonjour, j'attende la voiture que viens un peu plus tard. Priez de me dire quand elle arrive.
WAGSTAFF	Yes, I shouldn't be at all surprised. *(Exits upstairs.)*
	(POLIGNAC *goes to get a drink, sees there is no one to serve him so goes to ring the bell as* BETH *comes down the stairs.*)
POLIGNAC	Ah, mademoiselle vous êtes bien venue. J'ai été en train de sonner pour quelqu'un.
BETH	What?
POLIGNAC	Je voudrais quequechose à boire. Alors c'est possible?
BETH	What?
POLIGNAC	Allez me chercher quelquechose à boire, je ne demande pas de trop!

BETH	(*giggles, fascinated by this strange language and begins to egg him on to say some more.*) Go on, my dear.
POLIGNAC	Alors, on est chez des fous. Je n'ai jamais vu de pareil.
BETH	Go on, some more, my dear! (*Giggles.*)
POLIGNAC	J'en veux a boire ma fille. Vous comprenez — à boire. (*He mimes pouring out a drink and drinking it.*)
BETH	(*giggles louder.*) I can 'ear you don't come from these parts, me dear!
POLIGNAC	Eh bien, j'ai fais la manche pour la dernière-fois. Ma chère petite fille, j'en veux à boire—pas vous—moi! Vous comprenez. J'ai soif, je veux une boisson! Vous etes bien la bonne. Alors allez me chercher quelquechose et cessez de ronronner comme un chaufbain! (*By now almost screaming.*)
	(BETH *collapses with laughter.* POLIGNAC *throws his hands in the air and collapses on the sofa.*)
BETH	Don't stop, my dear. (POLIGNAC *maintains stony silence.*) Oh—come along, my dear. (*No response.*) What's the matter? Was it something I said?
POLIGNAC	Ma chère petite——
BETH	That's better. (*Laughs.*)
POLIGNAC	Ah mon dieu, allez-vous en!
BETH	Oh now, simmer down, simmer down. You'm much too excitable, 'ere, 'ave a drink and calm down. (*She goes to pour out a drink and* POLIGNAC *is overjoyed to think she's at last understood what he wanted.*)
POLIGNAC	Enfin. Ca y est. On est arrivé! Et il n'a fallu qu'une demi-heure. (*Literally on his knees with ironic gratitude.*)
BETH	(*thinking he must crave liquor.*) Oh I can see you'm an alchololican, my dear. (*Nervously pours out a drink and hands it to him.*)
POLIGNAC	Merci, Mademoiselle, merci.

BETH	Didn't even say thank you!
POLIGNAC	Combien.
BETH	What?
POLIGNAC	C'est combien? Oh ca va—laisse tomber. (*Holds up his glass to her saying 'cheers.'*) Santé.
BETH	(*thinks it's for her.*) Oh ta, just a drop. (*She takes a sip.* POLIGNAC *explodes.*) (*Looking bewildered.*) 'Ere you are.
POLIGNAC	(*takes the glass and pats her on the hand.*) Merci.
Beth	Oh! (*Obviously delighted. She giggles and holds out her hand to be patted again.*)
POLIGNAC	Eh encore! (*He obliges.*) (BETH *comes out from behind the bar. They are both now side by side in front of the bar and* POLIGNAC *has his elbow on the counter.*)
BETH	Ha—Ha—— (*Pats* POLIGNAC.)
POLIGNAC	Ha—Ha—— (*Nudges* BETH.)
BETH	Ha—Ha—— (*Nudges* POLIGNAC.)
POLIGNAC	Ha—Ha—— (*Chucks her under the chin.*)
BETH	Ha—Ha—— (*Chucks him under the chin.*)
POLIGNAC	Ha—Ha—— (*Slaps her on the behind.*)
BETH	(*outraged.*) 'Ere! (*She swipes at him and knocks his elbow away.* POLIGNAC *falls flat on his face.* BETH *rushes out in terror D. L.* POLIGNAC *picks himself up.*)
POLIGNAC	Les Anglais! (*Sits down on the sofa and picks up a magazine.*) (ALF *and* FLASH *enter.*)
ALF	All clear! That was a near one.
FLASH	Yes, 'ere look out, there's Poliygnack, Fred can't change with him around.
ALF	He'll just 'ave to sit tight in the bushes for a bit.
FRED	(*entering, still in his underwear and mackintosh.*) Eee, I'm frozen ——

(POLIGNAC *turns and smiles.* ALF *and* FLASH *smile back.*)

ALF	Take this case and change into your own things in the dining room.
FRED	Aye but he'll see——
ALF	We'll keep him talking. 'Urry up!

(ALF *and* FLASH *stand by* POLIGNAC *and screen him while* FRED *exits stealthily.*)

	'Ullo.
POLIGNAC	'Ullo.
FLASH	'Ullo.
POLIGNAC	'Ullo.
ALF	'Ullo.
POLIGNAC	Comment ca va?
FLASH	Don't change the subject.

(*Enter* DANBY.)

DANBY	Ah, Mr Tubbe, here's your French phrase book.
ALF	Oh, thanks.
DANBY	Can I help at all?
ALF	No, you can clear off for a bit.
DANBY	Good show. (*Sees* POLIGNAC.) Hullo.
POLIGNAC	'Ullo.
ALF	Don't you start.
DANBY	Start what?
FLASH	We've just had all that out.
DANBY	Oh. Have you seen Susan?
ALF	She's around somewhere.
FLASH	In the kitchen.
DANBY	Oh wonderful! (*Exits.*)
FLASH	What's so wonderful in the kitchen?

ALF	Now look, I'm going to be pretty busy 'ere, so go upstairs and don't let anyone down 'ere for a bit, OK?
FLASH	OK. But what about him? (*Points to* POLIGNAC.)
ALF	That's all right, he's goin' to 'ave a little snooze. (*To* POLIGNAC.) Aren't you? (*Nods and smiles.*)
POLIGNAC	(*nods and smiles.*) Oui.
FLASH	Can't I 'elp?
ALF	Don't be silly, we're not goin' to run any risk. Fred's goin' to do it for us.
FLASH	Oh, I got yer. (*Goes upstairs.*) You're a mastermind, Alf, a real genisis. (*Exits.*)
	(*Enter* FRED, *clothed once more.*)
ALF	That's better. Now then, Fred.
FRED	Now then, what?
ALF	You see this gentleman on my right?
FRED	Aye, 'Ullo.
POLIGNAC	'Ullo.
ALF	Not again! (*Then smiles at* POLIGNAC, *who smiles back.*) There's only this bloke standing between you and a fortune.
FRED	(*incredulously.*) Go on?
ALF	Remove him, and you'll 'ave affluence.
FRED	Alf who?
ALF	You'll be rich.
FRED	Oh, will I? Beth would like that.
ALF	Yes. Now we better nab him quick or it'll be too late.
FRED	Aye, but how?
ALF	Clock him one!
FRED	We might 'urt 'im. Couldn't we drug him with sleeping pills?

ALF	Have you got any?
FRED	Aye, I've got a bottle of asprin.
ALF	Don't be daft, we'd need about twenty to put him out.
FRED	It's a full bottle.
ALF	'Ow d'you think we'll get him to take twenty asprins?
FRED	You mean he might get a bit suspicious?
ALF	I don't know what I'd do without you, but I'd rather!
FRED	Oh thanks. Well, we'll knock 'im out, but where shall we dump him?
ALF	In there. (*Points to panel.*) Look, I'll talk to him, and you nip round behind and dot him one.
FRED	With what?
ALF	Use the rabbit punch.
FRED	What's that?
ALF	You know, like this.
	(*He does it on* FRED, *who crumples to the floor.*)
	For crying out loud, get up! Fred, Fred, get up!
	(*Stands him up and shakes him. Then sees* POLIGNAC *looking at them so pretends they're just having a good laugh and slaps* FRED'S *back.*)
	Fred! Wake up, you fool! (*Laughs.*)
FRED	(*coming round.*) What hit me?
ALF	Pull yourself together, it's me, Alf. (*Laughs.*)
FRED	What the 'ell are you laughin' at?
ALF	Nothing. How do you feel? (*Laughs.*)
FRED	Look, if you think it's funny——
ALF	Shut up, we're being watched, laugh, damn you, laugh!

FRED	(*laughs then holds his aching head.*) Don't know what I'm laughing at. You do the Frenchman in, you're good at it.
ALF	OK. You talk to him while I get behind him.
FRED	What shall I say?
ALF	'Ullo seems to please him as much as anything.
FRED	Right. (*Goes over to* POLIGNAC.) Er — 'Ulloooo.
POLIGNAC	Allo.
FRED	Eee, it works, I can speak French!
POLIGNAC	Pardon?
FRED	Ullooo. (*To* ALF.) Hurry up, I can't keep this up.
POLIGNAC	Je ne comprends——
	(ALF *delivers the blow and* POLIGNAC *collapses.*)
ALF	Quick, open the panel.
FRED	I can't, it's shut!
ALF	Kick the notch!
	(SUSAN *and* DANBY *enter from the kitchen.*)
DANBY	I say, sir?
ALF	What? Oh—er——
	(*Sits down beside* POLIGNAC *and pretends he's talking to him and answers for him too.*)
	—What do you want, Danby?
DANBY	Do you mind if we go out?
ALF	No, I'd love you to.
SUSAN	How's Mr Polignac this morning?
ALF	Oh fine, aren't you, oui, oui. (*Waves* POLIGNAC'S *hand.*)
SUSAN	Did he sleep well, after all that excitement?
ALF	No, not very. Non. (*Waves* POLIGNAC'S *hand again.*)

DANBY	I expect he'll have a little nap before his race.
ALF	Yes, he's looking a bit tired now.
DANBY	Well, cheerio, we shan't be too long.
ALF	That's all right.
SUSAN	Au revoir, Monsieur Polignac.
	(*Silence.*)
FRED	(*to* ALF, *whispering.*) That's you!
ALF	Eh? Oh — au revoir.
SUSAN	Vive le Cardinal!
ALF	(*waves* POLIGNAC'S *arm.*) Oui, oui.
	(DANBY *and* SUSAN *exit.*)
	I've aged ten years.
FRED	Aye, me too.
ALF	A lot of help you were; open the panel.
FRED	OK. (*Kicks beam, panel opens.*)
ALF	Come on, my sleeping beauty, in you go.
	(*They dump* POLIGNAC *in and shut the panel.*)
	Now there's no time to lose. (*Getting out French book.*) If you're going to take his place you've got to know something of the language.
FRED	Oh no, if I've got to open me mouth, it's off!
ALF	Stop arguing. Now let's see what you'll need to say.
FRED	'I am French' will do, won't it?
ALF	They know that. You want to tell them you don't speak English. 'Ere we are. 'Some Useful Phrases.' 'What time is it?'
FRED	Half-past ten.
ALF	Shut up. I'm reading.
FRED	Oh, well, I've got a watch so I don't need that.
ALF	'I have a puncture.' 'My handlebars are twisted.' 'Where is the Post Office?'

FRED	They'd be a great 'elp.
ALF	'My grandmother has missed the train.'
FRED	That's daft, isn't it?
ALF	Yes.
FRED	She's dead.
ALF	'My position has been struck by lighting.'
FRED	Never mind. It doesn't show.
ALF	Ah! 'Ere we are. 'I do not understand, speak more slowly, please.' That's all you need. (*Hands the book to* FRED.) Now you try it in French.
FRED	(*in a meaningless accent.*) I—do—not understand —speak—more—slow——
ALF	What the 'ell's all that about? Say it in French. It's written on the other side.
FRED	Oh! 'Jee—nee——'
ALF	Jeannie! (*Takes the book and looks.*) 'Jerr—nee! Jer—nee—comprehends pass—parles—plus—lent-ment. Sil—voos—plate.'
FRED	Doesn't make sense.
ALF	Doesn't have to, it's French!
FRED	I'll never learn all that.
ALF	Well, we'll cut it short. Just say. 'Please, I do not understand.' That's 'Sil—voo-plate —jer-nee—comprends pass.' Now try that.
FRED	Silv-er—plate-jer-nee—comm—com—com come again?
ALF	'Compronds pass.'
FRED	Oh aye. 'Comprends pass.'
ALF	Right, now again.
FRED	Sil-ver—plate. Jer-nee—comprends-pass.
ALF	Again, and faster this time.

FRED	Sil-ver—plate. Jew—nee compronds pass.
ALF	I don't know, there's something wrong somewhere—I know!
FRED	What?
ALF	It's yer 'ands.
FRED	Me what?
ALF	Yer 'ands. You've go to wave 'em about, see. Like old Polignack. Let's 'ave it again and use your 'ands this time.
FRED	Silver plate. (*Then starts his arms working like a windmill.*) Jer nee compronds pass!
ALF	No. No, that's too much. Try just one arm.
FRED	Silver plate——
ALF	Never mind the collection, get on with it!
FRED	(*with one arm revolving.*) Jer nee compronds pass.
ALF	Better, but it's not right. Keep your arm still, just move yer hand.
FRED	(*flipping his hand about.*) Silver plate. Jer nee compronds pass.
ALF	Ah, that's better, that's coming along a treat. Now then once more for luck.
FRED	(*with his arms stiffly to attention and at breakneck speed.*) Silver plate—jernee compronds pass!! Look, no 'ands!!
ALF	(*throws up his hands in disgust.*) Tell you what, don't open yer mouth at all. Just act dumb. (*Looks at* FRED.) Shouldn't be difficult. Now 'ave you ever been on a horse?
FRED	No.
ALF	Oh. Well, first of all we've got to make sure you know how to mount.
FRED	It's not mounting I'm worried about, it's staying on!
ALF	Once you're up there just 'ang on like grim death.

FRED	*For* a grim death, you mean.
ALF	It's getting on that's important. Now look, practise on this sofa. This is the head and that's the tail.
FRED	This is the head and that's the tail.
ALF	Yes.
FRED	Where's the startin' post?
ALF	There. (*Pointing ahead.*)
FRED	And the finishing post?
ALF	There. (*Points behind.*)
FRED	Eee, I'll 'ave to go backwards.
ALF	Course not, you go round in a circle. Now the first time you'll see the horse is after you've been weighed in.
FRED	Weighed in? I'm riding it, not fighting it!
ALF	Shut up! Right, now you'll come up and see it in the paddock. You can just give it a friendly pat on the quarters.
FRED	Ye—On the what?
ALF	The quarters.
FRED	Which quarter?
ALF	There's only one quarter
FRED	Don't be daft, there must be four quarters.
ALF	Yes, I think you're right. There's forequarters and hindquarters. Go to the hindquarters, they're about here. (*Indicates on sofa.*) You walk up, pat it, and say 'hullo' or something like that. In French, of course.
FRED	What's 'hullo' in French?
ALF	'Ullooo,' I think. Now come on, just try it. You're seeing it for the first time. Right?
FRED	Right. (*Walks up, looks around, suddenly sees the sofa and pats the end of it gently.*) Ullooo!

ALF	No, you want more confidence. You've go to let it see who's riding who.
FRED	Doesn't it know?
ALF	Come on now, firmer this time.
FRED	(*repeats the business with a swagger.*) Ullooo!
ALF	Go easy, you'll 'ave the RSPCA after yer! Now we come to the tricky bit. You've got to mount it.
FRED	I'll have a pair of steps.
ALF	Don't be daft.
FRED	I'll say we 'ave 'em in France.
ALF	No, listen! You come round to the left of the 'orse, put your left foot in the stirrup and swing the right leg over.
FRED	Sounds easy enough.
ALF	Well, come on, try it. Put your left foot in my hand.
	(FRED *does so.*)
	Now throw the right one over.
	(*He does so and shoots straight over the top.*)
FRED	Ow!!
ALF	Now you've gone and upset it. You'll 'ave to calm it down. (*He pats the sofa soothingly.*) There, there, there. Come on, pat its head.
FRED	There, there. I don't see why I should stroke him, he's just brained me.
ALF	It's your fault, it was standing quite still and you get it all excited.
FRED	There, there.
ALF	Whoa, whoa back.
FRED	Whoa there. Perhaps he'd like some sugar.
ALF	No, he's all right now.
FRED	I'm glad to 'ear it.

ALF	Now try again.
FRED	OK. Ready?
ALF	Yes.
FRED	Whoa, steady boy, easy, easy. Whoa!
ALF	What's up?
FRED	Flies are worryin' him.
ALF	Come on, urry up, the others are 'alf to the starting post by now.
FRED	Are they? (*He looks.*) Blimey, so they are. All right, 'ere we go.
ALF	Right. Now, one, two three up!
	(FRED *disappears over the back again.*)
FRED	Help!
ALF	Idiot, can't you hold on when you're up?
FRED	Hold on to what?
ALF	The reins!
FRED	There aren't any!
ALF	Well, can't you pretend? 'Ere, use your braces.
FRED	I 'aven't got any. Let's use yours.
ALF	Right 'ere you are. (*Puts his hands in his pockets. Lays the braces on top of the sofa.*) Now try again, Fred.
FRED	OK. Here goes. (*This time he stays on.*) 'Er it's quite comfy, just like the back of a sofa.
ALF	Got the reins?
FRED	Yus.
ALF	Well, use both hands.
FRED	I can't. I've got me phrase book in this hand.
ALF	Well, put it away.
FRED	Where shall I put it?

ALF   Don't tempt me, son. Now then, you're at the starting gate. I'm the starter. As soon as they're in line I'll pull the lever and they'll be away. Ready?

FRED   Aye.

ALF   Right — Now! (ALF *pulls an imaginary lever and his trousers fall down.*) They're off!

           (FIRE *enters and sees* ALF *and screams as the curtain falls.*)

Scene Three

The same. That afternoon. The radio is playing softly. ALF *is pacing up and down nervously, looks at his watch and then goes to pour himself a drink. He just takes a sip as* FLASH *enters through panel.*

FLASH   Whatcher!

ALF   (*chokes and turns.*) Don't do things like that, boy. I'm in a very nervous condition.

FLASH   Sorry, pal. Fred on the course all right?

ALF   Yes, we'ad a bit of luck with them sending that car for Pollygnack. I just bundled Fred in instead and away he went.

FLASH   Well, so long as he don't open his mouth we're OK.

ALF   Don't worry, he won't, he's too much to lose if they catch him out.

FLASH   Is the race on yet? (*indicating radio.*)

ALF   No, not yet.

FLASH   All right for me to stay and listen?

ALF   Yeh!

FLASH   'Ow about the Police?

ALF   She's gone, thank Gawd!

RADIO   This is the BBC Light Programme.

ALF   Sh!

RADIO   We are now taking you over to Seldon Park for
               a commentary on the Seldon Handicap.

FLASH   'Eere we go!

RADIO   Graham Dundunning will describe the race to
               you from the grandstand assisted by Jack Briggs
               as race reader so over to Seldon Park.

FLASH   I want a drink.

COMMENTATOR Good afternoon to you from Seldon Park and a
               perfect spring day it is too.

ALF   'Perfect!' That's all he knows. (*Bangs radio.*
               Volume down.)

               (ALF *and* FLASH *are now talking over the*
               commentary.)

FLASH   Now take it easy, Alf.

ALF   With ten thousand
smackers 'anging over me
head? Oh, I wish I was there!

FLASH   Don't be daft. No
sense in moving around the
scene of the crime. If anything
goes wrong we don't want to
be on the spot, do we?

ALF   No. (*Points to panel.*)
Polygnack still in there?

FLASH   Yus, he was snoring
sweetly as I came through.
Look, when it's all over what
are you going to do with——

ALF   Dry up, will yer? I'm
trying to listen!

COMMENTATOR   I don't think
we've had such fine weather for
the Seldon Cup since before the
war. There have been no
cancellations and all the runners
are the same as those mentioned
in your papers this morning.
There are ten in the race
altogether and now I'll just run
through the card for you. Berserk
trained by Smith, ridden by Nash,
drawn three. Orange Tree trained
by Block, ridden by Callow, drawn
two. Surf trained by Leith, ridden
by Turner, drawn six. Cardinal
trained by Monsieur Raymonde
and ridden by A Polignac, drawn
five. Blank Spot trained by Eves,
ridden by Brough, drawn seven.
Hasty trained by Addyman, ridden
by Holmes, drawn one. Penny
Plain trained by Barker, ridden by
Adams drawn four. New Year
trained by Dyson, ridden by G
Flood, drawn nine. City Lights
trained by Walter, ridden by

FLASH All right! All right! Blimey, it ain't started yet.

ALF Sh! (*Listening.*) Did he mention the Cardinal?

FLASH I dunno. I wasn't listening.

Fosbery, drawn eight, and Rainy Day, trained by Jones and ridden by J Dellar, drawn ten. Well, they're coming out on to the course now and going down to the start. Blank Spot is just going by, looking very fit indeed wearing red and green colours, followed by Hasty and New Year.

ALF Give me another glass. (*Bangs radio. Volume up.*)

(POLIGNAC *totters out of panel in a daze. He intercepts the glass as* FLASH *hands it back filled to* ALF. POLIGNAC *drinks it and puts empty glass into* ALF'S *hand and totters back into panel. and it shuts.*)

ALF (*drinks from the empty glass.*) That's better!

ALF Sh! Listen!

COMMENTATOR And here comes the favourite Cardinal.
He's looking magnificent, a beautiful chesnut. This is the first time his jockey, Polignac, has been to England, he's probably feeling a little strange.

FLASH I bet he is an' all!
ALF Sh!

I've got my glasses on Polignac now and he's certainly looking very determined, he seems almost glued to his seat.

ALF I wish he was.

There's certainly no doubt about Cardinal's ability, he was unbeaten in France last season, but he's got some stiff opposition here today. Both Berserk and New Year have won over the distance and according to their trainers they have every confidence in their ability to win.

ALF Thank Gawd for that. Cor, if we could have shoved in Sweet Lavender!

(*Volume goes down.*)

FLASH She's still in a coma.

ALF I know and whose fault's that?

Well, they're beginning to arrive at the starting gate now, so until they're under starter's orders, I'll just tell you a little about the race itself. The course is roughly in the shape of a 'U.' They go straight for about five furlongs and then there's a left-hand turn, another slight left-hand turn and the last four furlongs brings them up the hill to the finish.

FLASH You told us to dope it to keep it immobilized.

ALF Yes, but not paralysed.

FLASH If he gets to the starting post all right we've got nothing to worry about.

ALF Well, he hasn't, not yet!

FLASH Don't get jittery.

ALF I'm not. Gimme another drink.

(*Bangs radio. Volume comes up.*)

FLASH OK. (*His hand shakes as he pours out the drink and hands it to Alf, who is also shaking.*)

ALF Quiet. They've reached the start.

They're coming into line for the roll call now.

FLASH Won't be long now.

(*Enter* BETH *from kitchen. Volume goes down.*)

BETH 'Ere, where's my Frederick?

ALF (*engrossed.*) Just reached the starting post.

BETH What?

ALF Eh—Oh—er—he's busy.

Hasty, then Orange Tree, Berserk. He's giving a spot of trouble but Nash has got him under control again, then Penny Plain and next to him Cardinal, Surf, Blank Spot moving round a little. City Lights and on the outside there's New Year and Rainy Day. Well, it won't be long

BETH Where?

ALF Where?

FLASH He's gone over to watch the races.

BETH I've got the afternoon off. I could join him, couldn't I?

ALF You could try.

BETH He'd get proper surprise if I sat down beside him, wouldn't he?

ALF So would the 'orse!

BETH Eh? (*Exits.*)

FLASH He said 'of course.'

ALF Who the 'ell cares what they're wearing!

FLASH 'Ere we go! 'Ere we go!

ALF Now quiet!

FLASH Turn it up a bit!
      (ALF *turns radio up.*)

ALF Oh Gawd! Careful, Fred! Careful!
FLASH ⎱
ALF   ⎰ 'Ang on! 'Ang on!

ALF Idiot!

now before they're off. And you can sense the excitement in the crowd.

(*Volume comes up on* BETH'S *exit.*)

This fine weather has certainly brought out a colourful selection of the latest fashions in hats and dresses. It shouldn't take long to get this field of ten horses under way.

Oh, Penny Plain's come out of line, Adams seems to be having some trouble trying to coax him back again. He's stamping around a bit and he's upset Cardinal. I think he must have just kicked him slightly because Cardinal has reared up and Polignac is having quite a struggle to quieten him down—but he isn't succeeding and Cardinal seems to be trying to throw him.

It looks more like a rodeo. He's kicking his hind legs out and Polignac has got his arms tight round the horse's neck, but he doesn't look very safe to me. Well, this—— Oh, he's fallen off! Yes, Cardinal has thrown him. He's lying on the ground. I don't know if he's hurt or not. Someone's rushed over to him and they're

FLASH
ALF } Get up! Get up!

ALF   He'd better!

FLASH   Telling me!
(COLONEL WAGSTAFF *enters
through front door and stands just
behind* ALF's *chair and listens.*)

ALF   So'e oughter be!

ALF   Other side, you fool, get
the other side.
(ALF *leaps up and appears to
crack the Colonel under the chin.*
ALF *is too preoccupied to notice
and the Colonel totters down and
subsides on to the sofa unconscious.*
FLASH *is also far too busy to
notice.*)

ALF   Don't answer 'im!

FLASH   Keep your mouth
shut.

ALF   Thank Gawd!

helping him up gradually. He's
sitting up now and shaking his
head—I think perhaps he was
slightly stunned. Well, I
wonder if he'll be able to ride
after all this . . .
   It would certainly alter the
whole complexion of the race
if the favourite had to be
scratched.
   Oh, he's on his feet again
now and I think he's—yes,
he's going to remount.
Cardinal is standing perfectly
still again and looking almost
ashamed of his burst of
temper.

   Polignac still seems a bit
shaken and—oh, he must be
thoroughly dazed, he's trying
to mount from the wrong side.

(*Volume down.*)

What an extraordinary
beginning to a race but, of
course, it's always the
unexpected in racing that
makes it such an exciting and
unpredictable sport.

(*Volume up.*)

   As far as I can see the first-
aid man is talking to Polignac,
probably asking him if he feels
fit enough to carry on.
   The Frenchman obviously
doesn't understand, he's not
replying at all.

> In fact he's remounting—
> yes, from the wrong side but
> he's on again and Cardinal
> seems to have sobered down
> and he's moved back into
> line. All the other horses are
> standing quite still, so perhaps
> this time we shall be away.
> They seem to be in a straight
> line now and—They're off!

(*Radio goes dead.*)

FLASH	I've gone deaf in this ear.
ALF	Where are yer? (*To radio.*)
FLASH	(*taps radio.*) Wake up!
ALF	(*hits radio.*) Ruddy thing won't work.
FLASH	(*hits radio.*) What's the matter with it?
ALF	We got to know what happens. 'Ere, take my glasses and go to the course.
FLASH	Right.
ALF	Get near enough to see, but don't get caught.
FLASH	No. OK. (*Exits.*)
ALF	(*hitting radio.*) Come on, for Gawd's sake! (*Sees* COLONEL.) 'Ere, can you get this perishing thing working again? D'yer hear? I won't—'Er, wake up! (*Pats his cheeks.*) Wake up! Colonel, this is no time for a nap. (*Shakes him.*) Colonel, Colonel, Squad, shun!
COLONEL	What? (*rises with a start.*)
ALF	I want the radio on. It's not working. Look! (*Bashes it.*) See, it's gone off. I must have it. (*Hits it again.*)
WAGSTAFF	Oh, well, there may be a loose valve.
ALF	Well, tighten it. How do you get in?
WAGSTAFF	Now, let's see.

(*Enter* MRS WAGSTAFF *with tea-tray for four.*)

ALF   Hurry up, it'll all be over!

MRS W   Here we are, Henry, tea.

WAGSTAFF   Thank you, dear. (MRS W *puts tray down.*)

ALF   Shake it. (*Tries to do so.*)

WAGSTAFF   Now careful.

ALF   But I got to hear the race.

MRS W   Try putting it on its side.

ALF   Yes. (*Grabs it.*) What?

MRS W   The kitchen clock always works better that way.

WAGSTAFF   Don't be silly!

               (ALF *stands it upside down.*)

ALF   Speak to me. (*Hits it.*) Please!! (*Hits it again.*)

WAGSTAFF   I say, let me do it. (*Takes it.*)

ALF   Make the perisher speak.

MRS W   Mr Tubbe, do calm down. (*Hands him a cup of tea.*)

ALF   (*politely.*) Thank you so much. (*Gives it a kick.*)

               (*Radio comes on again.*)

RADIO   Orange Tree second and Penny Plain third.

ALF   Eh, what? Who was first?

RADIO   Cardinal first. Yes, after a magnificent race
               Cardinal was first, Orange Tree second and
               Penny Plain third.

               (*Radio crackles, squeaks and goes dead again.*)

ALF   (*about to explode.*) Fred, I'll—— (*Covers up quickly.*)
               Well, there's a turn-up for the book!

WAGSTAFF   Did he say Cardinal?

MRS W   Yes, that dear little man has won. Isn't it
               splendid?

ALF   Yerse.

Mrs W	When he gets back we must give him a very special reception.
Alf	Yes, we must.
	(Flash *dashes in.*)
Flash	Alf, Alf, the bloody fool—— (*Sees* Mrs W. *and* Colonel, *stops and raises his hat.*)
Mrs W	Oh, hallo, Mr Harold.
Flash	How do.
Mrs W	I don't think you've met my husband. This is Mr Harold, Henry.
Wagstaff	How do you do, Mr Henry.
Flash	Pleased to meet you, Mr Harold.
Mrs W	Do sit down and have a cup of tea.
Flash	No, I don't think——
Alf	(*pulling* Flash *on to sofa.*) He'd be delighted. Behave yourself. What happened?
Flash	He won.
Alf	I know he won, but how?
Flash	He just hung on and the 'orse did the rest, but that ain't all.
Mrs W	Your tea. (*Hands it to* Flash.)
Flash	Tar.
Alf	What you mean, that ain't all?
Mrs W	Sugar? (*Hands him bowl.*)
Flash	Tar. He hasn't stopped yet!
Alf	Eh?
	(*With sugar in one hand and cup in the other,* Flash *can't use the sugar tongs so after juggling round he pours the whole basin full into his cup.* Alf *retrieves one lump from* Flash's *cup and puts it in his own, licks the tongs and puts them in his breast pocket.*)
Flash	He never pulled up!
Alf	Where is he now?

FLASH	Gawd knows! He jumped the rails, went right through the crowds, then leaped over the hedge on to the main road. More like the Grand National.
MRS W	Cakes? (*Offering the plate.*)
FLASH	Tar. (*Lays his hand flat in the middle of the plate and gets it covered in sugar and cream, licks his fingers and then takes a cream horn, looks at it, and sucks it like an ice cream cornet.*) He was doing about sixty!
ALF	Why didn't you go after him?
FLASH	I couldn't, the cops were on his trail.
MRS W	Napkin? (FLASH *has his two hands full so puts the cake in his mouth, takes the paper napkin and mops his brow.* ALF *snatches it from him and puts it in his top pocket.*)
	(FLASH *then finds the tea too hot, so pours it in his saucer and is about to blow but thinks that's a bit common, so waves his hat over it instead.*)
FLASH	Police must 'ave rumbled something was up. What are we going to do, Alf? What are we going to do!!
	(COLONEL WAGSTAFF *has now come over with his cup of tea and sits on left arm of couch.*)
ALF	Don't sound so worried. (*Demonstrates to* FLASH *how to hold his saucer, ie sticking both his little fingers out into mid-air and* FLASH *drinks like that from the saucer.*)
FLASH	Smashing char!
WAGSTAFF	Yes, it is a bit strong though, dear.
MRS W	Is it? Oh, I forgot to bring the water. I'll go and get some. (*Exits.*)
	(FLASH *has had enough of tea, so while* COLONEL WAGSTAFF *is busily sipping he pours the remainder of his saucer into* WAGSTAFF'S *wellington boot.*)
	(WAGSTAFF *suddenly feels his wet foot, so gets up very slowly and goes off upstairs.*)
ALF	You mean to sit there with cream dripping off yer chin and tell me Fred never stopped.

FLASH	No, he just went sailing on. He's got half the countryside out after him.
ALF	Why the 'eck didn't you join in?
FLASH	What the 'ell could I 'ave done if I'd seen him?
ALF	You could have tripped him up or something!!
	(*Bangs the radio and it comes to life again playing the overture to 'William Tell.'*)
FLASH	'Ere don't you shout at me like that.
ALF	I'll shout if I want to.
FLASH	Just because you've made a mess of things——
ALF	I've made a me——. Whose idea was it to put a perishing 'orse in the cupboard, eh?
FLASH	Whose idea was it to lock up the Frenchman and put that raving idiot in his place, eh?
ALF	'Ere, can you hear anything?
FLASH	No.
ALF	Sure?
FLASH	Only the radio.
ALF	I'll swear I can hear 'orse's 'ooves.
FLASH	(*listens.*) No, it's drums.
ALF	You sure?
FLASH	'Course I'm sure.
ALF	Well, I'm not.
FLASH	If you don't believe me turn it off and see for yourself.
ALF	Right. (*Does so.*)
	(*They listen, shrug their shoulders. They both 'doubletake' as they realize it's not the radio.*)
FLASH	Blimey!
ALF	I told yer!
FLASH	Alf, d'yer think——
	(*The hooves come clattering to a stop. A horse neighs. There's a shout, followed by the sound of crashing glass and* FRED *enters through front door with bow legs. He looks muddy and half dead.*)

ALF }
FLASH }   Fred!

               (FRED *is past speech and collapses in the middle of the*
               room. ALF *and* FLASH *speak while trying to lift* FRED
               up.)

ALF   You blithering idiot, do you realize you've lost
               us ten thousand pounds?

FLASH   Ten thousand and you've probably landed us in
               gaol.

ALF   Not content with starting the race off with a
               circus act you have to win the perishin' thing!

FLASH   Why couldn't you stay at the back?

ALF   And stop when you got to the end?

FLASH   Who d'you think you are, Gordon
               Sir—flippin'—Richards?

FRED   I've had enough! I'm finished, I'm through!

ALF   The cops are after you.

FRED   I know. They chased me over half-a-dozen
               hedges and a couple of five-bar gates.

ALF   'Ere, Flash, we'll have to scapa. Open the
               panel. (FLASH *does so.*)

FRED   I'm not going in there again.

ALF   You'll do as you are told!

FRED   I won't!

FLASH   Listen, Fred. If the cops nab you, you'll land
               yourself in clink!

FRED   I don't mind. I might get a bit of peace.

               (POLIGNAC *totters out of panel in a dazed condition.*)

ALF   Don't talk wet.

FLASH   (*to* POLIGNAC.) Watcher! Now look here,
               Fred—where the 'ell's he come from?

ALF   Gawd! As if we 'adn't enough to worry about!

               (*Police whistle is heard.*)

FIRE (*off.*) Hold that horse. It's Cardinal.

ALF   Look out! The Police!

(FRED *is pushed behind front door, and* POLIGNAC *behind the bar.* FIRE *enters through front door.*)

FIRE   Have you seen a jockey?

ALF   He went that way. (*Points to French windows.* FIRE *dashes off.*) Here, Flash, if she wants a jockey, we'll give her one.

FLASH   Eh?

ALF   The real one. Come on, Fred.

FLASH   Oh, I get yer. (*Takes* FRED's *cap and silk.*)

ALF   (*to* POLIGNAC.) Time you got ready for the race. Oui? Race? (*Mimes riding.*)

POLIGNAC   (*in his daze.*) Ah, oui. (*Also mimes.*) Je gagnerai.

ALF   Catch on quick, don't yer?
(*Takes* POLIGNAC's *jacket of and helps him on with the silk.* FLASH *pulls one of* FRED's *boots and throws it to* ALF.)

FLASH   Now the other boot. (*Pulls the boot off and throws it to* ALF.)

ALF   'Urry up, she'll be back in a minute. (*Puts the cap on* POLIGNAC *and again mimes racing.*)

POLIGNAC   Merci. (ALF *rolls up* POLIGNAC's *trousers. Police whistle, off.*)

FLASH   Here we go. (*Pushes* FRED *out of sight and picks up boots. Enter* FIRE.)

FIRE   (*sees* POLIGNAC.) Aah!! the jockey!

ALF   We got him trying to hide the evidence.

FIRE   Stout work! Come on! (*Grabs him.*)

POLIGNAC   Merci. Bonjour, messieurs. Merci.

ALF   Good luck! (*Miming riding.*)

FLASH   'Ope you win.

(POLIGNAC *and* FIRE *exit.*)

ALF   Well, we're broke but safe. Let's pack our bags and go.

(*They start going upstairs.*)

FLASH   I think we better lay off 'orses for a bit.

ALF	Yes, but how else are we going to make an honest living?
FLASH	Well, how about forgery?
ALF	No, that's no good, we 'aven't got a forge. I've got it!
FLASH	What?
ALF	Boxing! Always fancied myself in the boxing racket! It's much easier to fix a fight than a race.
FLASH	Yes, we only need a mug who is not too old and can't box.
FRED	Aye. that's it. Now who do we know that's not too old and can't box?

(*Looks at* ALF *and* FLASH *who are looking at him.*)

Oh, no! No! No!

(*Rushes downstairs, followed by* ALF *and* FLASH *as the stairs collapse.*)*

CURTAIN.

*The author realises the difficulties involved in a 'collapsing staircase.' Towards the end of the London run there was an addition made to this final curtain. As Alf and Flash made a grab for Fred and the stairs collapsed, Alf got caught in the dry rot hole, the Colonel came back onto the balcony with his gun and in the general shouting and scuffling the gun went off. Fred, who by this time was on his way to the French windows, yelped and leapt into the air. Curtain.

The business with the gun might very well be used instead of a 'collapse.'

PROPERTY PLOT
Act I.

On Stage. Newspaper on table near front door.

Writing pad and pencil on table near front door.

Bottles of drink and glasses, etc, at the bar throughout play.

Off Stage. Breakfast tray and newspaper—Mrs Wagstaff

Scarf—Colonel Wagstaff.

Second breakfast tray—Mrs Wagstaff.

Jacket—Colonel Wagstaff.

Letter in pocket—Beth.

Shoe laces—Beth.

Suitcase—Beth.

Register—Mrs Wagstaff.

Black Homberg hat—Alfred.

Half-a-crown for tip—Flash.

Two suitcases—Fred.

Two suitcases—Beth.

Suitcases—Susan and Danby.

Act II, Scene 1.

On Stage. Newspaper on table near front door.

Off Stage. Attache case filled with sandwiches, sausages, and a flask—Fred.

Broom and duster—Beth.

Papers and account book—Danby.

Duster—Beth.

Parcels of shopping—Colonel Wagstaff.

Wristwatch—Alf.

Two letters—Alf.

Letters—Danby.

Suitcase—Polignac.

Act II, Scene 2.

On Stage.   Whisky and glass from bar.

Off Stage. Attache case, including food—Alf.

Homberg hat—Alf.

Gun—Colonel Wagstaff.

Gun—Beth.

Feather duster—Beth.

Homberg hat with hole in it—Alf.

Act III, Scene 1.

On Stage.   Red flag tied to bannisters.

Writing materials for Susan.

Broom—Beth.

Mail.

Magazine.

Off Stage. Breakfast tray—Mrs Wagstaff.

Breakfast tray—Susan.

Attache case and hat—Alf.

Mackintosh, and case containing jockey's outfit—Flash.

Grip—Polignac.

French phrase book—Alf.

Pair of braces—Alf.

Act III, Scene 2.

On Stage.   Portable radio.

Wellington boots worn by Colonel Wagstaff.

Off Stage. Tea-tray for four—with cups, saucers, etc, sugar bowl, bowl and sugar tongs.
Plate of cream horns—Mrs Wagstaff.

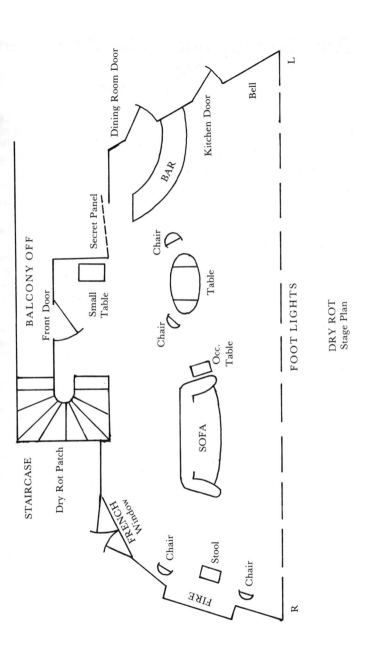

DRY ROT
Stage Plan